BASEBALL'S WINNING WAYS

J. D. Thorne

Good Hitting!

J. D. Thorne

Sporting Chance Press

Printed in the United States of America
Sporting Chance Press™, Inc.
Third Printing

ISBN: 978-1-7345863-3-6

Sporting Chance Press™, Inc.
1074 Butler Drive
Crystal Lake, IL 60014
sportingchancepress.com

The photographs and illustrations appearing in *BASEBALL'S WINNING WAYS* were sourced from the Library of Congress, David Bernacchi, Wikimedia Commons, and Bill Potter. Please see the Photographs and Illustrations Credit Table on page 179 for more information.

The opinions and ideas expressed are those of the author who is entirely responsible for its content. The author has composed *BASEBALL'S WINNING WAYS* at his own expense, using his own resources and technology.

Baseball Is a Beautiful Game

I look out the window to see my grandchildren tossing around a baseball. By their smiles, I can see they are having fun—just like their parents, grandparents, and great grandparents did before them.

Enjoyed in a variety of ways, baseball can be played with just a few players in *catch, running bases, home run derby, strike-out*, and *stickball.* If more kids are available, it can be played in neighborhood games at the park or with a full line-up in organized play.

The finest thing about baseball is that when it is taught and coached properly, players learn to improve in many ways. Players develop certain habits of good behavior. Some call these *virtues*, but most think of them as fundamentals or *principles*. Baseball players learn these principles when they are young.

With good coaching, principles are reinforced in practice after practice, in game after game. The greatest coach in *Major League Baseball* history, Joe McCarthy, called his principles the "10 Commandments of Baseball." Coaches have been using these for over 100 years, but few know about their origin!

Baseball's Winning Ways can be read by all fans age 12 and older. Readers will find topics that take them to new interests. Schools, home schools, and libraries will find this book helpful as well.

Baseball's Winning Ways discusses the history of the game and some famous players. This book touches on American history that took place while the game was played. And it includes a feature developed by founding father, Benjamin Franklin.

Key terms and phrases in *Baseball's Winning Ways* are noted in *italic* and explained in the glossary. A reader's quiz, discussion questions, and Winning Ways Charts will help readers get the most from this book.

CONTENTS

J. D. THORNE

Breaking Down Baseball by Eras

Let's look briefly at 150+ years of baseball according to different eras or periods of time. Breaking down baseball *chronology* by eras is helpful to understanding the sport although it is *subjective*. Scholars often review such breakdowns and refine them.

Early Pro Era (1869-1900)

Baseball was getting established. Rules were being set and people from different parts of the country started to play it in the same way. In this period, the first pro teams were formed and the American and National Leagues were created.

Dead Ball Era (1901-1919)

The Dead Ball Era took place during the first two decades of the 20th century. The professionals were focused on: 1) offense that was called *small ball*; 2) pitchers who threw spitballs; 3) a new *foul strike rule,* and 4) balls used for long periods of time during a game. All these led to low scores.

Lively Ball Era (1920-1945)

During the Lively Ball Era: Spitballs were banned, balls were more frequently changed during a game, and Babe Ruth and others began a period of power hitting that changed how players batted.

Post-War Era (1946-1960)

When World War II players returned to baseball after military service, naturally, the game improved. The leagues were integrated and the game was starting to get television coverage, which blossomed in the 1950s.

Former soldiers and their growing families tuned in and many attended ball games.

Expansion Era (1961-1973)

As the population continued to grow and people moved out west, some Major League Baseball (MLB) teams relocated and new teams were created. The National and American Leagues had eight teams for the first 60 years of the 20th century, but between 1961 and 1973, both leagues expanded to 12 teams. The expansion would continue. Today there are 15 teams in each league and 30 total in Major League Baseball.

Free Agency Era (1974-1985)

Players had played under restrictions that made it difficult for them to move from team to team. Negotiations between the players' union and Major League Baseball led to a new era of free agency.

Enhancement Era (1985-2010)

New ways of increasing performance through advanced training, diet, and other aids led to a period of experimentation. Major League Baseball had banned steroids, but did not test for their use until 2003. Their use grew until testing improved and penalties increased. Some players took steroids and used other treatments without understanding their exact nature or their long-term health effects. Other athletes played a cat and mouse game with Major League Baseball by attempting to stay just ahead of policing efforts. Certain cherished records were broken unfairly that hurt baseball's reputation. Major League Baseball has stepped up efforts to clean up performance, but it is an effort that requires constant vigilance.

Sabermetrics (2010-present)

Sabermetrics (baseball statistics) have an important role in team management today. Technology is king in the 21st century as applications, smart phones, and the "cloud" continue to take over our lives. Is it any surprise that statistics have played a much more important role in the way teams are managed? Teams want to make use of the best performance especially in key situations. Pitch counts, rest between pitching starts, understanding the exact value of a certain hitter or pitcher in a given situation—Sabermetrics have become an important management tool.

Baseball Cards

Trade cards were collectable cards that were given away when some products were bought. They would feature and promote products offered by certain *tradesmen*. Around since the 1700s, trade cards became more popular with color *lithography* in the late 1800s. The topics covered expanded from advertising messages to subjects of interest to consumers. These ranged from serious images of the U.S. presidents to humorous ones that gave exaggerated views of family life. There were cards with famous person *caricatures*, beautiful outdoor scenes, ships, Native Americans, and more. Like other types of advertising, some images were offensive for various reasons.

Baseball comes alive for fans because of the action and the personalities of the players. Original trading cards of baseball players came free with tobacco products. Eventually, they would become available on many different types of products like milk, cereal, and bread. Sold separately as well, they have been a kind of social media component of baseball since its early history. Fans have collected cards for fun. They talk about baseball cards. They trade baseball cards. Today, we use the term "trading cards" for baseball cards. For young fans, it's hard to imagine an easier way to learn about favorite players, teams, and the competition.

In *Baseball's Winning Ways* you will see biographies of some of the greatest baseball players in history along with some of the stars today. These are our "baseball cards" for this book. We also include drawings by Bill Potter that feature quizzes similar to those on classic versions of baseball cards.

The Players

Let's look at some of the great players from the past and some of today's stars as well.

Aaron, Hank

When she was very young, a neighbor of mine would sit on the living room carpet listening to the Milwaukee Braves games on the radio. Sometimes her dad would take her to a Braves game at Milwaukee County Stadium. One day, the great slugger, "Hammerin' Hank" Aaron, hit a ball that her dad was able to snatch in the stands. It was an awesome experience that she would never forget.

Like many baseball players, Aaron came from modest beginnings. In the earliest days of baseball, many athletic young boys came from the mills and factories looking for something better. Aaron was an African American player who came from the rural south and faced the added pressure of prejudice as he traveled around the country. Despite the difficulties, Aaron became one of America's most treasured athletes.

Aaron created many winning moments for baseball fans. Possessing a strong throwing arm, great strength, and quick wrists, he played in the outfield for most of his career. His career lasted from 1954–1976 and he played 21 seasons of it with the Braves, the first dozen in Milwaukee and then nine more in Atlanta after the team moved there. In his long time on the diamond, he hit an astounding 755 home runs, whacked 3,771 hits, and collected 2,297 RBIs. He played in 25 *All-Star games*, he was awarded three Gold Gloves, he won two *batting titles*, and he was named National League Most Valuable Player (MVP) in 1957. Aaron's 1957 Braves were World Series champions. He was one of those especially gifted players who hit for power and average. The Hank Aaron Award is given annually to Major League Baseball players selected as the top hitter in each league, as voted on by baseball fans and members of the media. Aaron was elected to the Hall of Fame in 1982.

Ruth, McGraw, Altrock, and Schacht

Altrock, Nick

Nick Altrock was a professional baseball player and left-handed pitcher. He won 62 games in his best years for the Chicago White Sox from 1904 through 1906. Altrock won Game 1 of the 1906 World Series versus the mighty Chicago Cubs.

The White Sox of 1906 was a team of modest hitters, so much so they were called the “Hitless Wonders.” The White Sox needed excellent pitchers like Altrock and his teammates Ed Walsh and Doc White.

It is hard to imagine today, but Altrock started performing funny clown routines while coaching first and third base. The fans loved him. He had an especially prolific career coaching, occasionally playing, and mostly clowning for the Washington Senators. He played in *vaudeville* and he was popular wherever he went. He entertained audiences into his 80s.

In the photo above, Altrock is doing some creative writing while sitting on his comedic partner Al Schacht with Babe Ruth and Manager John McGraw looking on. This type of photo would have been in newspapers all over the country.

Arenado, Nolan

Nolan Arenado is a third baseman for the Colorado Rockies. He is an intense player, a perennial All-Star, and a slugger. When he came into the league, he was loaded with potential, but he needed a lot of work on the field and in the weight room. He put the work in and the results followed: Seven Gold Gloves, five-time All-Star, *Wilson Defensive Player of the Year* for 3 years at third base, 3 years National League (NL) Platinum glove, four Silver Slugger Award winner, and top NL home run leader for three seasons. For the shortened 2020 season, Arenado's batting performance suffered, but he did hit a respectable .253. He is the best fielding third baseman in the Majors. Arenado is the leader in assists, putouts, and turning double plays over several full seasons at third base. Many believe he is the finest third baseman of his time.

Banks, Ernie

Ernie Banks played his entire career with the Chicago Cubs. During his long playing career, the Cubs were never competitive until his last few seasons. In 1969, the team was ahead in the National League East all the way to mid-September when a losing streak took the team out of the pennant race.

Throughout his career, Banks was one of the Cubs players that drew fans to Wrigley Field. He became known as "Mr. Cub." Early in his career, he had five seasons where he hit more than 40 home runs. In two of those, he was the top home run hitter in baseball.

In addition to his playing, Banks will forever be remembered for his positive attitude and how he looked forward to every game. He often suggested "let's play two" and the fans loved him.

Banks played from 1953–1971. As a shortstop, Banks was the National League Most Valuable Player in 1958 and 1959. He was the Cub's first *Gold Glove Award* winner in 1960. In response to injuries that made shortstop difficult, Banks became first baseman for the Cubs in 1962. In 1970, Banks hit his 500th career home run at Wrigley Field. Banks retired from playing in 1971 and was the first Cubs player to have his uniform number retired in 1982. For Banks' career, he had 512 home runs, 2,583 hits, and a .274 batting average. A stop by the Statue of Ernie Banks at the entrance to Wrigley Field is a favorite pursuit of fans on a visit to Chicago. Banks was inducted into the Baseball Hall of Fame in 1977.

Bell, James Thomas "Cool Papa"

African American "Cool Papa" Bell was a great hitter and terrific fielder. Had the "color barrier" not existed in his youth, there is little doubt that he would have played in the Major League because of his blinding speed on the base paths, if nothing else. Although he declined the opportunity, he was offered the chance to play for the St. Louis Browns at age 48 in 1951. His roommate, Satchel Paige, often told the story that Bell was so quick he could turn out the light and be in bed before the room got dark!

Although a genuine star, he was an unselfish man. In 1946, he deliberately allowed another player, Monte Irvin, to win the league batting title because it would help Irvin attract a Major League contract offer, which Irvin ultimately earned with the New York Giants.

Bell earned his nickname for his composure under pressure as a 19 year old pitcher in 1922 at the start of his career. He played for the Homestead Grays, the Pittsburgh Crawfords, the Kansas City Monarchs, and the St. Louis Stars over a 28-year career. He was inducted into the National Baseball Hall of Fame in Cooperstown, New York, in 1974.

Bender, Charles Albert "Chief"

Chief Bender was an excellent pitcher who played 16 years in the Majors. Raised on the White Earth Indian Reservation in Northwest Minnesota, he was the son of a German-American settler and an American Indian mother thought to be from the Ojibwe tribe. His parents had many children and they lived in a cabin on a farm on the reservation.

Bender was an intelligent man devoted to baseball. After his long playing career, he coached for many years in the Minor Leagues. He also coached at the United States Naval Academy.

Bender was known for his intelligence and his competitiveness. He watched for weaknesses in opposing hitters. For most of his career, he played for the Philadelphia Athletics for Manager Connie Mack. Many writers covering baseball mentioned Bender's Indian heritage and used "creative wordplay" to describe his exploits. Fans *followed suit* during games and although Bender may have been well-liked, generally a baseball player wants to be judged on his playing. When it came to playing, he delivered on that score. Bender played from 1903–1917. Then as a coach with the White Sox in 1926, he came off the bench one day to pitch.

As a player, the 1910 season was a particularly good one. He was 23–5, with a .821 winning percentage; an earned run average (*ERA*) of 1.58; and he pitched a near perfect no-hitter in which a base on balls was his only mistake of the game.

Bender won the opening game of the 1910 World Series that would lead to Philadelphia's first world championship. The following 1911 season, Bender and the Athletics were in the series again, this time playing against the New York Giants. Three times in the series, he was on the mound, capturing two wins with the A's winning another Championship. In 1913, he and the A's faced the Giants again in the series. The great pitcher won another two games and the A's another Championship. Bender was a sportsman who also enjoyed hunting, bowling and golf.

He continued to manage, coach, and scout late in life. Bender had many hobbies and worked in the sporting goods field as well. In 1953, Bender was inducted into the Baseball Hall of Fame.

Berra, Lawrence Peter "Yogi"

Despite his many baseball records, "Yogi" Berra will be remembered for his humor. Berra is famous for his sayings that are called Yogisms such as "it ain't over 'til it's over" and "when you come to a fork in the road, take it." Berra was courageous, funny, and irreplaceable.

Berra was a Major League Baseball catcher and manager. He played for the New York Yankees from 1946-1963, one of their best periods. In Berra's 19-year baseball career, he was an All-Star fifteen seasons, a three time AL MVP, and a 10-time World Series champion. A great handler of pitchers and a clutch hitter, Berra was inducted into the Baseball Hall of Fame in 1972.

Betts, Markus Lynn "Mookie"

Betts is one of the most exciting players in baseball. Drafted by the Red Sox in 2011, Betts began his big league career in 2014. Starting at centerfield, Betts moved to right field in 2016. He also plays second base. Betts played six seasons for the Red Sox.

Betts was the 2016 Wilson Defensive Player of the Year for right field and the Overall Defensive Player of the Year that season. In 2018, Mookie Betts became the first player in Major League Baseball history to win the Most Valuable Player, Silver Slugger, Gold Glove, batting title, and World Series in the same season. The 2018 Red Sox won the Series by beating the Los Angeles Dodgers in five games.

Now Betts is the right fielder for the Dodgers. The Dodgers signed Betts to a long term contract that puts him at the top of the pay scale for the foreseeable future.

Betts has hit 155 home runs. His career batting average is .301 and career on base percentage is .373. His slugging percentage is .522 and his on-base plus slugging is .895. In addition to his batting skills and his ability to cover a lot of ground in the field, his arm is one of the best in baseball. His highlights reels show him robbing batters of hits and throwing out runners from deep in the field.

In the shortened 2020 season, Betts hit 16 home runs and batted .292. Playing a crucial role in the 2020 playoffs, he helped lead the Dodgers to their first World Series Championship since 1988! At the beginning of the season, Betts encouraged his team to do everything well all the time. In the playoffs, he excelled in fielding, base running, and hitting.

Betts is also a professional bowler for the Professional Bowlers Association (PBA).

Boudreau, Lou

Inducted into the National Baseball Hall of Fame in 1970, Lou Boudreau was an excellent player and successful Major League manager who later became a television broadcaster. Sportswriter Red Rennie used *hyperbole* to describe Boudreau in this way: "He can't run and his arm is no good, but he is the best shortstop in the game." Boudreau may not have been the most gifted athlete, but he applied great discipline and intelligence to make the most of his skills and achieve success. He was also referred to as someone who played and managed with "class."

Boudreau played from 1938–1952. He was made player/manager of the Cleveland Indians in 1942 at the age of 24. Boudreau's 1948 Indians beat the Boston Braves in the World Series. He retired with a .295 batting average. He won the American League batting title in 1944, the 1948 Major League Player of the Year, and the 1948 American League MVP. Lou Boudreau remains the only manager to win a World Series and win the Most Valuable Player Award in the same season. He had an astute understanding of the game at an early age.

Brown, Mordecai "Three Finger"

Mordecai "Three Finger" Brown was a superb pitcher who played from 1903–1916. At age 7, his hand was damaged in a farm accident, but he had the courage and fortitude to work with his affliction. After much practice, he developed the ability to throw pitches with great ball movement. Many articles were written about Brown's great work-effort and the adjustments he made to become a success on the field.

The fine pitcher played nine of his seasons with the Chicago Cubs during one of their strongest periods. In 1906, Brown posted a 1.04 ERA with 26 wins and 6 losses. He helped lead the Cubs to the World Series title in 1907 and 1908. He had a career record of 239–130, with a 2.06 ERA and 55 shutouts. Brown was inducted into the Baseball Hall of Fame in 1949.

Bryant, Kris

Born in Las Vegas, 6-foot-5 Kris Bryant has played a winning hand for the Chicago Cubs. Bryant was the 2015 National League Rookie of the Year, the 2016 National League Hank Aaron award winner, and the 2016 National League MVP.

The third baseman and outfielder was a key member of the Chicago Cubs that defeated the Cleveland Indians in the 2016 World Series. It was the Cubs first Series Championship since 1908. The victory put an end to the so-called "Curse of the Billy Goat" and the Cubs stigma as "Lovable Losers." Bryant hit two home runs in the seven-game series. The three-time All-Star continues to make his mark on the game although in the shortened 2020 season, Bryant suffered from a number of injuries and played in only 34 games.

Cabrera, Miguel "Miggy"

Miguel "Miggy" Cabrera is the designated hitter and first baseman for the Detroit Tigers who is a two-time American League Most Valuable Player, four-time AL batting champion, and 11-time All-Star. Cabrera was a Triple Crown winner in 2012. He has won the Hank Aaron Award as the best hitter twice.

Coming up through the Minor League system for the Florida Marlins, his Major League career began in 2003. That year, the Marlins would go on to win the World Series. After five seasons, Cabrera was traded to the Detroit Tigers. In his Triple Crown season in 2012, he led the AL with a .330 batting average, 44 home runs, and 139 runs batted in.

Cabrera has hit 30 or more home runs in 10 seasons. He has driven in over 100 runs in 12 separate seasons.

Generous and community-minded, Cabrera has been nominated six times for the Clemente Award. In the shortened 2020 season, Cabrera batted .250.

Cobb, Ty

Ty Cobb was a superb outfielder who played Major League Baseball from 1905–1928. The son of a school teacher, Ty Cobb was an intelligent young man but showed more passion for baseball than biology. Cobb played during the "*dead ball era*" and he was superb at what would be called "*small ball.*" But when he broke into the game, he was a raw talent who needed instruction and practice, practice, practice. His perseverance and supreme effort made him a great player. He not only developed his fielding, but he worked on his sliding likely more than players before him or since.

He loved to beat out bunts and ground balls for hits. Once on base, he was determined to make the most of it. Cobb led the AL in stolen bases six times.

Cobb won the Triple Crown in 1909 and was the American League Most Valuable Player in 1911. Upon his retirement, he held several records: 3,035 games played, 11,429 at bats, 2,246 runs, 4,191 hits, 5,859 total bases, and a .367 batting average. Famous for an aggressive style of play, Cobb had 897 stolen bases. On six occasions in his career, he got on first base, stole second base, then third base, and then stole home. Cobb stole home 55 times! Although he retired over 90 years ago, his career batting average of .367 is still a record.

A highly-paid player in his time, Cobb used his money wisely and made excellent investments. According to players in his time, Cobb could be cantankerous, but his personal faults were sometimes exaggerated by others for profit in print. Cobb was inducted into the Hall of Fame in 1936.

Collins, Eddie "Cocky"

Eddie "Cocky" Collins played from 1906 to 1930 in the Major League. He was one of the most accomplished all-around ballplayers. "Cocky" was a confidant ballplayer and a college graduate. He played, coached, and then became a general manager.

Starting in 1906, he played for 25 years. In those days most batting titles went to Ty Cobb, but Collins beat Cobb for most stolen bases four seasons and for runs scored, 1912–1914. He had 3,315 career hits. He was a member of Connie Mack's Philadelphia Athletics "*$100,000 Infield.*" Anticipating a bidding war for his players from the new Federal League, Mack sold Collins services to the Chicago White Sox in 1915. Collins starred in the 1917 World Series victory over the Giants. In 1918, he joined the US Marines to serve in WWI, but returned the following year as one of the honest players on the 1919 "Black Sox" who had seven players that had taken a bribe from gambling interests to intentionally lose the World Series to the Cincinnati Reds. He was later named team manager for the 1924 and 1925 seasons. He finished his playing career back with Connie Mack's Philadelphia A's, also serving as third base coach for the 1929–1931 World Series champions. He then served as General Manager for the Boston Red Sox and signed Hall of Famer, Ted Williams. Collins was inducted into the National Baseball Hall of Fame in 1939.

Conlan, Jocko

Jocko Conlan was the son of a Chicago Policeman and the youngest of nine children. Living in the neighborhood around White Sox Park, young Conlan dreamed of being a professional baseball player. He played Minor League ball for roughly a dozen years and finally made it to the Majors with the Chicago White Sox for the 1934-1935 seasons. When an umpire passed out from the heat, he took his place and that duty led to his career in umpiring. First, he was sent down to the

Minors to ump. Then he worked his way up to the Big Leagues. He worked as a baseball umpire from 1941–1965. During his career, he officiated five World Series and six All-Star games. Conlan combined a smiling personality with a firm sense of authority. He wore a polka dot bow tie. Conlan was known to never curse a ballplayer. Inducted into the Hall of Fame in 1974, the game would not be the same without great umps like Conlan.

Clemente, Roberto

Roberto Clemente was a Puerto Rican of African descent who played right field 18 seasons for the Pittsburgh Pirates from 1955 through 1972. He joined the Marine Corp Reserves in 1958. Clemente came into the league just 8 years after Jackie Robinson had broken the color barrier.

Like many Americans, he played baseball for many hours a day. He watched pros who played in the area for the winter league and he would mimic their motions. As a youth, he was known for long hits, spectacular catches, and a great throwing arm. He was fast as well. In high school he was a high-jumper and threw the javelin. All his athletic pursuits helped him prepare for baseball.

Clemente was signed with the professional league in Puerto Rico where Major League players would play during the winter months. When Clemente started to play in the Majors, he was known for his near-reckless pursuit of the ball at the outfield wall. As a member of the Pittsburgh Pirates, Clemente had a difficult time laying off bad pitches.

Pittsburgh was not very good for many of the years in which Clemente played. However, in 1960, the Pirates compiled a 95–59 record during the regular season, winning the National League Pennant. They defeated the New York Yankees in a seven-game World Series. Back again in 1971, the Pirates compiled a 97-65 record, winning the National League Pennant, and defeating the Baltimore Orioles in seven games in the World Series. Clemente was named World Series MVP.

An All-Star for 12 seasons, Clemente batted over .300 for 13 seasons. He was a Gold Glove Award winner for 12 consecutive seasons. He had 3,000 hits during his career. He was the National League Most Valuable Player in 1966. He was the NL batting leader for four seasons. Clemente was a confident baseball player with a big heart. Involved in charity work in Latin American and Caribbean countries during the off-seasons, he died in a plane crash at the age of 38 while traveling to deliver aid to earthquake victims in Nicaragua.

Clemente's death was a watershed moment for American baseball. Major League Baseball renamed its annual Commissioner's Award in his honor; now known as the Roberto Clemente Award, it is given to the player who "best exemplifies the game of baseball, sportsmanship, community involvement and the individual's contribution to his team." Clemente was inducted into the National Baseball Hall of Fame in 1973.

Darvish, Yu

Born in Habikino Japan, Yu Darvish's services were acquired by the Texas Rangers where he played from 2012 through mid-season 2017. The 6-foot-5 220 pound Darvish was traded to the Dodgers where he played for the rest of 2017 and then signed with the Cubs in 2018. Darvish's first few years were outstanding for the Rangers, and he has rekindled that kind of performance for the Cubs in 2020. For the shortened 2020 season, Darvish had 8 wins and 3 losses to lead the league and an ERA of .201.

Like no other time, Major League Baseball has scouts all over the world looking for players who can be lured to the league in their youth!

DiMaggio, Joe

About one year after Babe Ruth retired from baseball, another great slugger began his career with the Yankees, Joe DiMaggio. DiMaggio was a quiet man who was completely dedicated to baseball like his coach Joe McCarthy. DiMaggio played for 13 years with the Yankees and had a superb career. He was selected for the All-Star team every season he played. DiMaggio was known for his fielding and his hitting. Some believe he was the best all-around player. He played centerfield for the Yankees and fans loved to watch how he could anticipate where a ball was going a split second after it was hit. He covered a lot of ground gracefully.

Like Babe Ruth, DiMaggio was a huge celebrity. For two months in 1941, DiMaggio got a hit in 56 consecutive games—a baseball record that many people believe will never be broken. At the time, as the hitting streak got longer, DiMaggio's most recent hit was the top news story of the day on the radio (TV did not exist) and in practically every newspaper. Fans huddled over their radios for news of every game as the amazing streak continued. It seemed like all of America was in suspense each day during that period. A popular song was made about "Joltin' Joe DiMaggio" performed by Les Brown and his Orchestra, and sang by Betty Bonney. DiMaggio was inducted into the National Baseball Hall of Fame in 1955.

Fox, Nellie

In 1947, Nellie Fox began his Major League career at age 19 for Connie Mack's Philadelphia Athletics. He was traded after the 1949 season to the Chicago White Sox where he would play for 14 seasons. By 1951, Fox had been an All-Star for 11 seasons in a row. A tough out, he had 791 walks set against only 216 strikeouts. Second base requires great defensive skills and Fox demonstrated those throughout his career.

It was well into Fox's career when the Gold Glove Awards were first presented in 1957. Fox was the first recipient of the award in the American League at second base. Fox would win two more Gold Glove Awards in 1959 and 1960.

In 1959, Fox played a critical role in the pennant winning season of the "Go-Go Sox." Fox hit .306 and captured the American League MVP award. Fox was inducted into the National Baseball Hall of Fame in 1997.

Josh Gibson and the Homestead Grays

Gibson, Josh

Although he died young at age 35, Josh Gibson amassed an amazing record of baseball accomplishments while playing in the Negro Leagues. He was revered at the time as one of the most powerful hitters in the game. He is shown in the Homestead Grays 1931 Championship photo above, top row, sixth from left.

His professional career began at age 18. He was known as an outstanding semi-pro player in Pittsburgh. One summer evening in 1911, he attended the first night game between his hometown team, the Homestead Grays, and the renowned Kansas City Monarchs. Poor lighting caused the pitcher and catcher to mix-up the signals. Expecting a slow breaking ball, the catcher instead got a blazing fastball. Catching it injured the catcher's hand, forcing him out of the game. So the Homestead Manager asked Gibson to come in as a substitute. Gibson was signed the following day to his first professional contract!

Over his career, he often led the league in home runs, but he also hit those for amazing distances. He blasted one that was measured at 575 feet! In one game at Yankee Stadium he hit a ball two feet from the top of the back wall behind the centerfield bleachers about 580 feet from home plate! It was estimated that if the ball had cleared the wall it would have rolled 700 feet. He was also an excellent catcher with a strong throwing arm who was a superb handler of pitchers.

Gibson had a fun-loving personality and was well-liked. Many considered him the greatest player in the league in his time. In 13 completed seasons, he won nine home run titles and four batting average championships. Among baseball experts he is considered the greatest catcher to play in the Negro Leagues. In 1972, Gibson was inducted into the National Baseball Hall of Fame.

Gehrig, Lou

Lou Gehrig held the longest consecutive game playing streak, 2,130, a record for over 50 years. Gehrig was a teammate of Babe Ruth and like Ruth he was also a big slugger. Gehrig was a quiet disciplined athlete. He took good care of himself and his exercise program was *commendable*. In one game, he hit four home runs. He held the record for most grand slams; he hit an incredible 23 "*round-trippers*" with bases loaded. He won the *Triple Crown*, which is the award for a player who leads the league in home runs, runs batted in, and batting average in one year. Gehrig played from 1923–1939.

Gehrig was nicknamed the "*Iron Horse*" because he was so strong and durable—like a steam engine. He is greatly admired for how he faced *adversity*. While Gehrig was still playing for the Yankees, he became ill with a disease called amyotrophic lateral sclerosis (*ALS)* that made him weak and unable to continue. Just a few months after he had to quit baseball, he was honored at a special appreciation day in Yankee Stadium. About 42,000 fans came out to see him and he was given many beautiful gifts. The speech he gave on that day is one of the most *legendary* speeches of all time. Although Gehrig was very sick, he said, "I consider myself the luckiest man on the face of the earth." Telling the crowd how lucky he was to play baseball, he thanked his teammates, family, and coaches. A popular movie was made about Gehrig called "Pride of the Yankees."

Gehrig's career numbers were outstanding: .340 batting average, 493 home runs, 1,995 RBIs, and a .632

slugging percentage. In 1939, Gehrig was inducted into the National Baseball Hall of Fame.

Griffey Jr., Ken

After his senior year at Moeller High School in Cincinnati and a stellar athletic career that included football and basketball, Ken Griffey Jr. was named U. S. High School Baseball Player of the Year. Griffey is the son of former MLB star Ken Griffey Sr.

In the June 1987 Baseball Amateur Draft, Griffey Jr. was the first player chosen in the first round by the Seattle Mariners. Griffey Jr. justified that confidence in his ability with a 22-year career spanning over four decades playing mostly for Seattle and then for his hometown Cincinnati. Over that career he was an All-Star 13 seasons. He hit 630 home runs, the seventh most all time in Major League Baseball history. He was also outstanding defensively winning 10-straight "Gold Gloves" in Center Field. He was named American League Most Valuable Player in 1997. In 2016 he was inducted into the National Baseball Hall of Fame. Although playing in an era where some players used steroids to artificially enhance performance, Griffey did not.

However, despite all his promise and glory, none of it might ever have happened. This is because after his first year in Minor Leagues, Griffey Jr. became depressed. "The coaches yelled at me during the season and when I came home my father and my family yelled at me too." Feeling he could not meet everyone's expectations, he attempted suicide. Fortunately, his girlfriend's mother discovered his attempt. She got him to the Hospital just in time to pump out his stomach of the pills he had taken, saving his life.

Henderson, Ricky

Rickey Henderson was a speedy left fielder who played for 25 years, from 1979–2003. His first start was with the Oakland Athletics where he played from 1979 to 1984. Henderson returned to the A's for three more stretches in his long career. He also played for the New York Yankees, the Toronto Blue Jays, the San Diego Padres, Anaheim Angels, New York Mets, Seattle Mariners, Boston Red Sox, and Los Angeles Dodgers. Henderson loved the game and he kept playing as long as he could.

An excellent lead-off hitter, many say the best, Henderson had a good average and he drew plenty of walks. He always gave pitchers a lot to think about whether up to the plate or on the base path. He made the most of every opportunity.

Henderson holds the Major League career record for career stolen bases, runs, and leadoff home runs. He is second, behind Barry Bonds in career bases on balls. Henderson was a ten-time All-Star. He was a Gold Glove recipient in 1981. In 2009, he was inducted into the National Baseball Hall of Fame. Baseball statistician and writer Bill James wrote this about Henderson: "If you could split him in two, you'd have two Hall of Famers."

Hornsby, Rogers

Temperance was one of the virtues that Rogers Hornsby practiced—he did not drink alcohol or smoke cigarettes. He believed a ballplayer could achieve what the ballplayer set out to accomplish. When he began his career for the Saint Louis Cardinals in 1915, he was a skinny 5-foot-11, 135-pound infielder. He worked on a farm during the offseason and gained weight for the new 1916 season. Hornsby played from 1915-1937. He played for the St. Louis Cardinals, New York Giants, Boston Braves, Chicago Cubs, and St. Louis Browns. Hornsby became one of the greatest right hand hitters. He is considered by many to be the best second baseman of all time.

Hornsby was a contemporary of Babe Ruth. Like Ruth, he was one of the greatest hitters. Hornsby hit .400 three times. He led the National League in batting seven times. He was named the National League's Most Valuable Player in 1925 and 1929. Hornsby accumulated a .358 lifetime average, second only to Ty Cobb. He batted .424 in 1924. As a player/manager, he led the Cardinals to their first World Series title in 1926. He was inducted into the National Baseball Hall of Fame in 1942.

Jackson, Reggie

Reggie Jackson was a right fielder who earned the nickname Mr. October for his clutch performances in the baseball playoffs. He played from 1967–1987 and was an American League All-Star for 14 seasons. Jackson has 563 home runs for his career. For 1973, Jackson won the American League MVP Award, the Major League MVP, and the World Series MVP Award.

In 1969, playing for the Oakland Athletics, Jackson had an astounding 34 home runs by July 5. The press saw his performance as one that might rival Roger Maris's 61-homer season in 1961. It was lights, camera, action from that point on. He ended the year with 47 home runs, his career best. He would never get any closer to Maris's record. But Jackson had plenty more highlights for the next 18 seasons.

Playing for the New York Yankees in Game 6 of the 1977 World Series, Jackson walked the first time out, but when facing Dodger Bert Hooton in the fourth inning, he lined the first pitch into the lower right field seats. In the fifth, he drove a pitch by Elias Sosa into the same area. On his next at bat against Charlie Hough, once again he hit a home run on the first pitch and it landed close to the others. Jackson was inducted into the National Baseball Hall of Fame in 1993.

Jeter, Derek

Coming from a highly educated and disciplined family whose parents met in the military, young Derek Jeter was asked to sign a contract each year that pointed out what behavior was acceptable and what behavior was unacceptable. He spent most of his youth in Kalamazoo, Michigan. His maternal grandparents had a large family in New Jersey so each summer he would spend time with his mother's brothers and sisters. He grew up as a very competitive athlete and Yankees fan.

Jeter's New York Yankee career spanned from 1995 to 2014. The 6-foot-3 shortstop was drafted out of high school in 1992 by his favorite team, the New York Yankees. The start of his career was not easy. He played for 4 years in the Minors. At times, his fielding was poor, but with determination, good coaching, and a terrific work ethic, he improved to big league standards and beyond. Finally, on opening day in 1996, Jeter was the starting shortstop. He kept that job for 17 seasons. In 1996, the Yankees would win the World Series for the first time since 1981. The Yankees would go on to win it again in 1998, 1999, 2000, and 2009.

Jeter was an excellent Major League shortstop and superb hitter. And he played better when he was most needed. Jeter played in 2,747 games collecting 3,465 hits, 1,923 runs, a .310 career batting average, 1,311 RBIs and 260 home runs. He had 358 stolen bases and five

Gold Gloves. In 2006 and 2009, Jeter won the Hank Aaron Award as the American League's top hitter.

Jeter is also one of the most popular players in recent history. In 2018, an Upper Deck 1993 Derek Jeter rookie card sold at auction for a grand total of $99,100—the most at the time a modern card had ever yielded.

One thing that speaks volumes about a former player is the number of other players who refer to him as their childhood idle. Jeter gets the nod from many today. Jeter was inducted into the National Baseball Hall of Fame in 2020.

Johnson, Randy

Pitchers can be downright scary to bat against when they throw at 90+ miles-an-hour. Certainly, Randy Johnson fit that bill. When you have a dominant pitcher like Johnson on your team, it is a definite bonus! On days when Johnson pitched, thousands more fans would show up to see him.

Johnson was a left-handed pitcher who played from 1988 to 2009. Nicknamed "The Big Unit," Johnson was 6-foot-10 inches tall and he threw a fastball that could exceed 100 miles per hour. The distance from the pitcher's mound to home plate is 60-feet-6 inches, but it must have seemed a lot closer when batters were up against the lanky pitcher. An All-Star 10 times, Johnson led the league in strikeouts nine times. In earned run average, winning percentage, and complete games, he led the league four times each. Johnson's career record was 303–166 with 4,875 strikeouts. Johnson pitched two no-hitters including one that was a *Perfect Game*. The Big Unit was inducted into the National Baseball Hall of Fame in 2015.

Johnson, Walter

Walter Johnson was the son of a Kansas farmer. According to the Baseball Hall of Fame, Johnson said a baseball felt natural in the palm of his hand and everything came together when he threw it. At 6-foot-1, tall for his time, Johnson was nicknamed "The Big Train" by poetic sportswriter *Grantland Rice*. The Kansas farm boy threw a blistering fastball.

Johnson played for the Washington Senators from 1907-1927. They were not a good team until 1924-1925. Johnson played in many games where he didn't get much offensive support from teammates. In fact, he pitched 64 1–0 games, winning 38 and losing 26. In 1924, the Senators beat the New York Giants for the World Series crown. The Big Train and the Senators were back at it again in 1925, but the Senators lost the series to the Pittsburgh Pirates.

After his playing career was over, he managed the Senators from 1929-1932 and the Pirates from 1933-1935.

The Big Train had 10 straight 20-win seasons and he had 11 seasons with a sub 2.00 ERA. Johnson had a career record of 417-279 and 2.17 ERA. His 3,509 strikeouts were a record for over 50 years. Johnson was inducted into the National Baseball Hall of Fame in 1936.

Keeler, Wee Willie

Wee Willie Keeler was a 5–foot–4 140 pounds third baseman and outfielder who could consistently "hit 'em where they ain't." Keeler batted over .300 for 13 straight seasons. He had a career batting average of .341. He was fast on the base path, a master at bunting, and one of the best place-hitters of all time. Keeler had

30 inside-the-park home runs and 495 career stolen bases.

He had a streak of eight consecutive years with 200-or-more hits—that held the record for 100 years. And he had a 44-game hitting streak that stood until Joe DiMaggio beat it. Keeler was inducted into the National Baseball Hall of Fame in 1939.

Kershaw, Clayton

The Los Angeles Dodgers are the league leaders in attendance with roughly 4 million fans attending games each season. The Dodgers organization has been one of the best in baseball, but they had not won the World Series since 1988 until 2020. One of the Dodgers best players since 2008 is pitcher Clayton Kershaw.

Kershaw has won three Cy Young Awards, five NL Pitching Titles (lowest earned run average in the league), one NL MVP, one Major League Player of the Year, one Branch Rickey Award in recognition of his exceptional community service, one Roberto Clemente Award for combining good play with strong work in the community, three Sporting News Pitchers of the Year awards, and the Triple Crown for Pitchers in 2011 for leading the league in wins, strikeouts, and ERA.

Kershaw threw a no-hitter at Dodger Stadium on June 18, 2014. The game was called by legendary sports announcer *Vin Scully*. Moments after the game ended on a strikeout, Kershaw's wife came on the field and Scully said: "When it is all said and done, he will escape all the excitement in the world and talk about a dream come true with his wife Ellen—a big moment in a young life."

In the shortened 2020 season, Kershaw marked up 6 wins and 2 losses. Kershaw helped the Dodgers advance to the World Series against the Tampa Bay Rays.

The Dodgers won the Series in 6 games with Kershaw winning two of them!

A likely future Hall of Famer, Kershaw, and his wife Ellen have established a foundation called Kershaw's Challenge that seeks to serve vulnerable and at-risk children.

Koufax, Sandy

Sandy Koufax was a pitcher who played from 1955–1966. He played for the Brooklyn Dodgers that moved to become the Los Angeles Dodgers in 1958. Koufax's first six seasons were statistically mediocre. The last half of his career was outstanding.

In Koufax's last five seasons, 1962-1966, his record was 111—34. He led the National League in earned run average each year; his ERA was under 2.00 in 1963, 1964, and 1966. He struck out more than 300 hitters in three seasons, including a record 382 at the time in 1965 for pitchers after 1900. Only Nolan Ryan has more strikeouts in a year with his mark of 383 in 1973. And in Koufax's final season, he was 27—9 with a 1.73 ERA, striking out 317 batters in 323 innings pitched, completing 27 of his 41 starts.

Koufax was an All-Star for six seasons, the National League's MVP in 1963, three-time Cy Young Award winner, and three-time National League Triple Crown pitching award recipient. Koufax has four World Series rings and he has two World Series MVPs.

Of Jewish faith, when the opening game of the 1965 World Series fell on Yom Kippur, the Jewish Day of Atonement, Koufax decided not to pitch it and the honor fell on the Dodgers other ace, Don Drysdale. Koufax did go on to pitch three games in the series, winning two of three games including the final one.

The great left-hander retired at the top of his game. His career was cut short because of arthritis. But during his last five final seasons, some believe he was the best. Koufax, a quiet private man, was inducted into the Hall of Fame in 1972.

Lasorda, Tommy

Tommy Lasorda was a pitcher who played for the Brooklyn Dodgers and the Kansas City Athletics in the mid-1950s. While not well known in his playing days, Lasorda went on to manage the Los Angeles Dodgers from late in the 1976 season to midseason 1996. Lasorda had a great managing career and won four pennants and two World Series titles. He was inducted into the National Baseball Hall of Fame in 1997.

One of the more colorful MLB managers, Lasorda was often asked to appear on television shows and in movies. After managing, he continued to work for the Dodgers in various capacities. Often a guest on baseball television programs, Lasorda was one of the more quotable baseball experts of the 20th century. Lasorda is known for his love of the Dodgers and Italian food.

Lombardi, Ernie

Catcher Ernie Lombardi was a big man, 6-foot-3 and 230 pounds, with a strong arm and an outstanding bat. But he was slow on the base paths. So slow, infielders would play way back. The powerful catcher compensated by hitting line drives. He also gripped the bat differently–he interlocked his hands.

The son of an Italian immigrant grocer, Lombardi played in the Majors from 1931-1947. Starting with the Brooklyn Robins his first year, he moved on to the Cincinnati Reds for a decade. He played for the Boston

Braves in 1942 and then finished out his career with the New York Giants from 1943-1947.

Lombardi played in two World Series for the Reds. In 1939, the Reds were swept in four games by the Yankees, but in 1940 they beat Detroit, four games to three. Lombardi won the National League batting title in 1938 and 1942. He was the National League MVP in 1938.

In 1945, Lombardi had the most putouts as a catcher in the National League. He was an All-Star seven times. Lombardi was inducted into the National Baseball Hall of Fame in 1986.

Luzinski, Greg

Greg "the Bull" Luzinski was a powerful and beloved left fielder of the Philadelphia Phillies from 1970-1980. He might have become a professional football linebacker had he not chosen a baseball career.

In his rookie season in Philadelphia, Luzinski whacked a home run that bonged off the replica Liberty Bell atop the center-field stands at old Vet Stadium 500-feet away from home plate! At the Phillies home today at Citizens Bank Park, towering 100 feet above street level, a new Liberty Bell rings after every Phillies home run.

After 11 seasons in Philadelphia, Luzinski played designated hitter for the Chicago White Sox.

In 1978, Luzinski won the Roberto Clemente Award given to honor a player for combining good play with strong work in the community. In 1981 and 1983, he won the Edgar Martinez Award as the best designated hitter in baseball. Luzinski retired with 6,505 at-bats, 307 home runs, 1,128 RBIs, and a .276 batting average.

CURVEBALL QUIZ
What Kalamazoo kid rocketed to fame with 1998, 1999, 2000, 2009 World Series Champion Yanks?
ANSWER ON FOLLOWING PAGE

[Curveball Quiz Solution: Derek Jeter]

Mack, Connie

Connie Mack was a giant in baseball history. Born during the Civil War, his 11 year Major League playing career was unremarkable in the 19th century, but his managing career from 1894 to 1950 was noteworthy! He managed the Philadelphia Athletics for 50 years.

Baseball's Hall of Fame lists Mack as manager, treasurer, and part owner of the Athletics. The A's were the first dynasty of the American League, winning six of the league's first 14 pennants. The Athletics won World Series titles in 1910, 1911, 1913, 1929, and 1930. Mack faced occasional tough financial times that forced him to sell off many of his best players.

Based on his long years as manager and his need to sell off players and rebuild teams, Mack's influence on player development was *unparalleled*. Mack's style of management was unusual in that he was considered the kindest and most soft-spoken of men. Mack was inducted into the National Baseball Hall of Fame in 1937.

Maddon, Joe

Joe Maddon has been named Most Valuable Manager in the American League and Most Valuable Manager in the National League. Said to be patient with his team on the one hand and cutting edge on the other, Maddon ranks as one of the best. He is sometimes referred to as "Joe Cool."

Maddon is the manager of the Los Angeles Angels (for the second time) after previously managing the

Tampa Bay Rays and the Chicago Cubs. Maddon's leadership on the field gave the Cubs their first World Series championship in 108 years in 2016. The Cubs beat the Cleveland Indians in seven games.

Maddon's teams have won 1,278 games and lost 1,102 for a winning percentage of .537.

Mantle, Mickey

For decades, the New York Yankees had at least one great slugger. It began with Babe Ruth. Lou Gehrig was the quiet star who played with Ruth and a few years after him. Joe DiMaggio then "stepped up to the plate" with Mickey Mantle "in the *batter's box.*" When Mantle came of age in professional baseball, his career was followed in newspapers, radio, and television. This small town boy from Oklahoma would be seen in many media outlets and in places like the cover of *Time Magazine.*

New York sluggers entertained each generation of fans. New York fans were passionate. Much was expected from these players.

Mantle is considered to be the greatest switch-hitter in baseball history. He played for 18 years from 1951–1968. Mantle was selected to the All-Star team for 14 years consecutively. In 1956 he won the American League *Triple Crown.* Mantle had 536 home runs during his career and holds many World Series records: 26 extra base hits, 18 home runs, 40 runs batted in, 42 runs scored and more. The Yankees won seven World Series championships during Mantle's career. Mantle was inducted into the National Baseball Hall of Fame in 1974.

Maranville, Walter "Rabbit"

Walter "Rabbit" Maranville was a shortstop who played for 23 seasons (1912-1933 & 1935). For his career, he had a .258 batting average, 2,605 hits, 1,256 runs, 884 RBIs, and 291 stolen bases.

But Maranville was someone who flirted with disaster. The Rabbit liked to goof around too much. For much of his career, he practiced very little self-control.

Players careers are wrecked when they drink too much, take drugs, or fall prey to other harmful behaviors. On the baseball diamond, Maranville was known for his superior fielding, tracking down grounders, and leaping to catch line drives. He was also a show-man with his basket style catches of fly balls that amused the crowd.

Off the field, Maranville was a hotel ledge walker, a goldfish swallower, and a practical joker who made good press for the newspapers, but was tiring for those trying to manage a baseball team. After nine seasons with the Boston Braves, Maranville was released.

After playing for a few different teams, he was picked up by Branch Rickey, the General Manager of the Saint Louis Cardinals. Rickey was an exceptional baseball leader and he wasted no time before he sent Maranville down to the Minors. He was giving him an opportunity to straighten himself out. Maranville decided for himself that he hit rock bottom. He quit drinking and had another seven strong seasons that earned him induction into the National Baseball Hall of Fame in 1954.

Mathews, Eddie

Eddie Mathews spent most of his 17-year Major League career (1952-1968) with the Braves of Boston, Milwaukee, and Atlanta. The only Brave to play in all three cities, the commanding left-handed hitter was a gifted third baseman with a strong arm needed for the "*hot corner.*" He teamed up with Hank Aaron to torture opposing pitchers facing the Braves from 1954-1966. Along with some great pitching, Matthews and Aaron led the Braves to two World Series against the Yankees—winning the title in 1957 and the runner-up spot in 1958. Late in his career after the 1966 season, he was traded to the Houston Astros where he played most of 1967 and then finished up his career in Detroit playing for the World Series champions in 1968.

Mathews had 512 career homers, a .271 batting average, 354 doubles, 72 triples, 1,453 RBIs, 68 stolen bases, 1,444 bases on balls, a .376 on-base percentage and a .509 slugging percentage. He hit 47 homers in 1953, a record for a third baseman at the time that got Mathews a lot of attention early in his career. He was a 12-time All-Star. He led the National League in walks four times. He finished his career with a .959 fielding percentage playing primarily at third base.

Mathews coached the Braves during three seasons from 1972-1974. He later worked for the Oakland Athletics organization as a hitting instructor. In 1954, the Braves third baseman graced the cover of the first-ever issue of *Sports Illustrated* magazine. Mathews was inducted into the National Baseball Hall of Fame in 1978.

Mathewson, Christy

Everyone liked Christy Mathewson. Mathewson was a professional baseball pitcher known by players and fans as a gentleman. He was tall and handsome, attended college at Bucknell, and wrote six books. Baseball players in the early 20th century were sometimes perceived to be carousers with little discipline and even less manners. A great churchgoer,

Christy Mathewson

Mathewson had given his mother assurances that he would not play baseball on Sunday. The papers reported on his good character. Mathewson was sometimes called in to advise officials on baseball problems and controversies. Mathewson got along well with his manager, one of the toughest men in baseball history, John McGraw.

A fan favorite, when Mathewson took the mound to start a game, he was warmly received with applause and cheers. Mathewson was a superb player who pitched for 17 seasons with the New York Giants. Mathewson won 373 games and he had a career 2.13 ERA while striking out 2,507. During World War I, he served in the army as a captain. Mathewson was inducted into the National Baseball Hall of Fame in 1936.

Mays, Willie

Willie Mays was one of those baseball players that Americans loved because he loved everything about the game. Many believe Mays was the best all-around player ever. Mays played the outfield flawlessly, earning 12 Gold Gloves. Mays was quick on the base path. He stole 338 bases. A great hitter, he had a .302 career batting average with 3,283 hits, 660 home runs, and 1,903 runs batted in. Mays had two seasons in which he hit over 50 home runs.

Mays was also spectacularly entertaining. His signature basket catches made him a joy to watch in the field. He might deliver a long ball at any at-bat. And he often stretched hits for an extra bag with his determination and speed. Mays was one of those players who made the game fun for everyone watching.

Mays played from 1951–1973, most of his career for the Giants who moved from New York to San Francisco in 1958. He finished out his career with the New York Mets in 1972-1973.

Like many sports heroes, Mays was someone who many young players imitated. His influence on American culture goes way beyond the baseball field. Mays was awarded the Presidential Medal of Freedom in 2015 by President Barack Obama. Mays was inducted into the National Baseball Hall of Fame in 1979.

Molina, Yadier

Yadier Molina is a catcher for the St. Louis Cardinals. A smart team-leader who is good for the clubhouse and a great strategist for pitchers.

He has played his entire career with the Cardinals. Molina is the recipient of nine Gold Gloves. He is a nine-time NL All-Star and a NL Silver Slugger Award winner. He is a two-time World Series champion—2006 and 2011 with the Cardinals. In 2020, Molina reached 2,000 career hits. Winner of the Roberto Clemente Award, Molina is a player who combines good play with solid work in the community.

In the shortened 2020 season, Molina batted a respectable .262. Molina's Cardinals were ousted in the 2020 Wild Card Series against the Padres, but Yadi batted .462.

Molina's older brothers, also catchers, Bengie (13 years) and José Molina (15 years) had successful careers in the Major League. Each brother has a World Series ring.

Morgan, Joe

Joe Morgan was one of the best second baseman in baseball. Although only 5-foot-6, he was strong and powerful. For 22 years, Major League fans watched Morgan on the diamond; he played 10 seasons for the Houston Colt .45s/Astros and eight seasons for the Cincinnati Reds. Morgan's career batting average was

.271; his on base percentage was .392; and his slugging percentage was .427. He had 2,517 hits; 268 home runs, and 1,133 RBIs. Morgan is ranked 11th in career stolen bases with 689.

While playing for the Cincinnati Reds "Big Red Machine," Morgan won back-to-back MVP awards and the Reds won back to back World Series in 1975 and 1976. The Reds of the 1970s were one of the best teams in baseball history. The second baseman finished out his career with the San Francisco Giants, the Philadelphia Phillies, and the Oakland Athletics. Morgan won five Gold Gloves and he was a 10-time All-Star. Morgan was inducted into the National Baseball Hall of Fame in 1990.

Musial, Stan

Stan Musial was a tremendous force for good in baseball and life. He ranks among the very best players of all time. One of thousands of good athletes from humble roots, Musial never forgot baseball fans for their support. Taking time out to sign autographs, chat, and acknowledge his fans, "Stan the Man" had a good sense of humor. He was a joy to be around.

Musial started playing for the Saint Louis Cardinals in 1941. His career is one of excellence and consistency. He held the highest batting average in the National League in 1943, 1946, 1948, 1950, 1951, 1952, and 1957. An All-Star for 20 years, Musial played for 22 seasons and he holds a career batting average of .331. He hit 475 home runs, 725 doubles, and 177 triples. He finished his career with 1,951 RBIs and 1,949 runs. A tremendous clutch hitter, he was fast in the field as an outfielder and on the base path. Musial was inducted into the National Baseball Hall of Fame in 1969.

Musial was famous for playing his harmonica, which became a trademark for him. He played it when he was out in public to amuse fans and he played it at hospitals when visiting the sick. He played his rendition of "Take Me Out to the Ball Park" at the National Baseball Hall of Fame. He also played his harmonica on the TV show, "Hee Haw."

Musial appeared on a number of TV shows such as the sitcom "That Girl" with Margo Thomas, the "*Ed Sullivan Show*," and "*What's My Line.*" Musial graced the cover of eight *Sports Illustrated* issues. President Lyndon Johnson named Musial National Director of the President's Council on Physical Fitness. Musial received the Presidential Medal of Freedom from President Barack Obama.

Niekro, Phil

Inducted into the baseball Hall of Fame in 1997, "Knucksie" is the greatest knuckleballer in MLB history. Pitching mostly for the Atlanta Braves, Niekro was able to get the hitters out with his patented pitch, the knuckleball. His mastery of it allowed him to successfully pitch in the Major League through age 48.

His success did not come from being able to throw a hard fastball or a sharp slider, but from throwing a slow yet darting pitch that was equally hard to hit. He is the oldest player to regularly play in the Major Leagues. He was the winning pitcher in 318 games. At age 43 he won 17 games and lost only four for the Atlanta Braves. At age 45 he won 16 games with only eight losses for the New York Yankees. Known also for his charitable work, in 1979, he won the Lou Gehrig Memorial Award for his exemplary character and in 1980, the Roberto Clemente Award for outstanding community involvement.

Posey, Buster

Buster Posey played several sports as a boy before going to Florida State University where he focused on baseball. Originally, he pitched and played shortstop, but moved to catcher and first base at FSU. Selected by the San Francisco Giants in the first round of the 2008 MLB draft, Posey spent a couple seasons in the Minor League. Posey played first base and catcher for the Giants in 2010 and he was named NL Rookie of the Year. It was a special year for Posey as the Giants proceeded through the playoffs and they went on to win the World Series with the rookie catcher.

After a 2011 injury, Posey came back strong in 2012 when he led the league with a .336 batting average, won the NL batting title, won the Hank Aaron Award for top hitter in the National League, and was named the NL MVP and the Comeback Player of the Year. The Giants won another World Series as well when they swept the Detroit Tigers in four games. In 2014, Posey and the Giants would win another World Series—this time against the Kansas City Royals. In 2016, Posey won a Gold Glove Award. Posey has been an All-Star for six seasons.

Posey and his wife, Kristen, adopted twins in 2020. The twins were premature with weakened immune systems so Posey made a decision to sit out the 2020 season due to the COVID-19 (Coronavirus) Pandemic.

Rickey, Branch

Branch Rickey was a lawyer and baseball executive. Rickey played in the American League as a catcher for the Saint Louis Browns in 1906 and the New York Highlanders in 1907. After managing the St. Louis Browns, he worked for the St. Louis Cardinals as president, field manager, and then general manager. In Saint Louis, he is credited with the development of the *farm system.* He persuaded Cardinals' owner Sam Breadon to buy stock in two Minor League teams giving the Cardinals first choice of players moving up to the Majors from those teams. Under this system, Rickey and the Cardinals won nine league championships. Naturally, the successful affiliation between Major League teams and Minor League teams spread to other organizations.

Rickey left the Cardinals to become president and general manager of the Brooklyn Dodgers in late 1942. Rickey created connections with black players that allowed him to scout untapped talent and led to desegregation in Major League Baseball. In October 1945, he signed infielder Jackie Robinson for the Dodgers' Minor League organization. Robinson's success with the Dodgers from 1947 led other owners to seek black talent. Rickey later was vice president, general manager (1950–55), and chairman of the board (1955–59) of the Pittsburgh Pirates. Rickey was inducted into the National Baseball Hall of Fame in 1967.

Ripken Jr., Cal

Cal Ripken Jr. played in 2,632 consecutive games, surpassing Lou Gehrig's record of 2,130. Nicknamed the "Iron Man," Ripken was a baseball shortstop and third baseman who played 21 seasons (1981–2001) for the Baltimore Orioles. Just as Gehrig is remembered fondly for his contributions to the game, so too is Cal Ripken Jr.

Drafted by the Orioles in 1978, Ripken signed a Minor League contract with the organization. Ripken started in the Majors in 1981, but was sent back down to the Minors for most of the season. Back in Baltimore late in the 1981 season, he was back on the roster from the start in 1982 when he won the AL Rookie of the Year Award as a shortstop. He originally played third base, but was moved to shortstop by Manager Earl Weaver. In 1983, the Orioles won the World Series and he was named the AL MVP.

In 1991, Ripken was an All-Star, the All-Star Game MVP, the AL MVP, and he won a Gold Glove Award.

For his career, Ripken accumulated 3,184 hits, 431 home runs, and 1,695 RBIs. A 19-time All-Star, Ripken won two Gold Glove Awards. Ripken was the AL Most Valuable Player twice. He won the Lou Gehrig Memorial Award in 1992 given to the Major League Baseball Player who best exemplifies the spirit and character of Lou Gehrig. In 1992, he also was presented with the Roberto Clemente Award.

For the final 5 years of his career, Ripken switched back to third base. In 2001, Ripken was named the All-Star Game MVP. He was honored with the Commissioner's Historic Achievement Award. Ripken holds the record for most home runs hit as a shortstop (345). He was named the starting shortstop for the Major League Baseball All-Century Team. In 2007, Ripken was inducted into the National Baseball Hall of Fame.

Robinson, Brooks

Perhaps the best defensive third baseman ever to play, Brooks Robinson, was born in Little Rock, Arkansas, in 1937. That same year, the Lamar Porter Boys Club Athletic Field was under construction by the *Works Progress Administration (WPA).* As a kid, Robinson worked in concessions at the field and played there.

Robinson played for the Baltimore Orioles for 23 years, from 1955–1977. Out on the field, Robinson put on a clinic for other infielders and superb entertainment for the fans. An 18-time All-Star, he won 16 consecutive Gold Glove Awards. The Orioles won two World Series championships (1966 and 1970) with Robinson on third. He batted .267 and hit 268 home runs in his career. In 1964, Robinson was awarded the American League MVP honors. In 1966, he won the All-Star Game MVP Award.

In 1970, he was the World Series MVP. He hit .429 with two home runs and six RBI for the Series. Robinson was inducted into the National Baseball Hall of Fame in 1983.

Robinson was known as a consummate good guy in baseball. He signed autographs willingly, was polite with the press, and generous with his praise for his teammates. Robinson was also generous to others. Many of his sports collectibles were sold at auction with proceeds going to charity.

Gordon Beard, longtime sports reporter in Baltimore, expressed the town's love for the star suggesting that "no one named a candy bar after him, they name their children after him."

Robinson, Jackie

Jackie Robinson was not only a great player, but his role in baseball was important for all Americans. Very early on, prejudice prevailed in baseball and blacks were shut out of the Major League game beginning in the 1880s. At the same time going back to the mid-1800s, there were black baseball teams and a few early leagues that were called Negro Leagues. In the 20th century, there was much activity and notoriety in the Negro leagues. There were All-Star games and a negro-league World Series.

There were a few Major League Baseball officials who wanted to see integration in professional baseball. One of them was Branch Rickey. Rickey had played baseball. He held many jobs in baseball and in late 1942 he was named president and general manager of the Brooklyn Dodgers. Later, he was also given a 25% stake in the club. An inventive-creative person, Rickey had several ideas that would make baseball a better game—one of those was to integrate the league. Rickey had several strategies for this effort, but perhaps of most importance was scouting and selecting the best men to cross the color line. He wanted men of great strength of character who would be able to take a lot of verbal abuse and stand up strong, but to hold back on their anger. He also wanted great players who could show Major League Baseball fans what they were missing. Among the men he chose was Jackie Robinson.

It should be noted that Jackie Robinson was no *shrinking violet*. He had several experiences with prejudice in his life and he was good at standing up for himself. But Rickey believed that the way to beat prejudice in the sport of baseball was to show your ability and toughness on the field—not fight with bigots in the stands. Only Robinson would understand the price he paid for paving the way for others in Major League Baseball and in society generally. No books can convey it, no second hand accounts explain it. And for Robinson the battle for equality and justice would continue for the rest of his life.

On April 15, 1947, Robinson made his Major League debut at Ebbets Field. For the 1947 season, the rookie played in 151 games where he had 175 hits scoring 125 runs. He had 12 home runs, 48 RBIs, and a .297 batting average. He had 29 stolen bases. Robinson was named the winner of the first Baseball Writers' Association of

America Rookie of the Year Award. In 1949, he was named the National League Most Valuable Player after leading the league in hitting with his .342 average and 37 stolen bases. In Robinson's 10 seasons, the Dodgers were frequent *contenders*, winning the 1955 World Series title and six pennants.

Robinson retired with a .311 batting average, 947 runs scored, 1,518 hits, and 197 stolen bases over 10 seasons. Robinson was inducted into the National Baseball Hall of Fame in 1962.

Ruth, Babe

Babe Ruth is one of the most famous people of all time. When playing baseball, the Babe was known around the world. Babe Ruth was a big, strong, fun-loving baseball player who hit more home runs than people thought possible.

Ruth's childhood was sad. His parents had eight children, but only Ruth and a younger sister survived childhood. His mother and father were tavern owners on the Baltimore waterfront. As a young boy, Ruth had a hard time behaving himself. His parents sent him to St. Mary's Industrial School for Boys in Baltimore. At this orphanage, Brother *Matthias Boutlier*, a 6–foot–6, 300 pound kind giant worked hard to help Ruth. Brother Matthias taught him how to play baseball. Once Ruth started playing baseball, he knew what he wanted to do.

Babe Ruth, New York Yankees, 1921

Ruth started out as a pitcher. When he played for the Boston Red Sox, he pitched a record of 29 scoreless innings in World Series play. Ruth's record stood until it was broken by Yankee pitcher Whitey Ford in 1961. Once Ruth began playing for the Yankees, he soon gave up pitching and concentrated on hitting.

Ruth played during the *Roaring 20s* and into the *Great Depression.* He held most hitting records during his playing time. He hit over 50 home runs in four different seasons. He hit a record 60 home runs in 1927. For his career, he hit 714 home runs. He hit at least 40 home runs in each of 11 seasons and led the league in home runs for 12 years. His career slugging percentage is .690—the highest of any player.

Ruth's Yankees were World Series champions four times. In Game 3 of the 1932 World Series, Ruth was said to have "*called his shot*" when he pointed towards the centerfield stands just before hitting a homer to the spot.

Ruth had a natural talent for sports, but his diet and lifestyle were a problem. He became sick and people started to believe that his career was finished. He improved his habits, his diet, and his exercise program. That helped him recover. He played 22 seasons. Ruth was one of baseball's *luminaries.*

It was not until 1961 that Ruth's home run record was broken. Roger Maris of the Yankees hit 61 homers that season. Ruth was one of the first members inducted into the National Baseball Hall of Fame in 1936.

Ryan, Nolan

Nolan Ryan was a 12th round selection in the 1965 draft by the New York Mets. After a brief Minor League stay, Ryan was promoted to the Majors at 19 years old in 1966, dropped down to the Minors, and then came back to stay from 1968–1993. He played for 27 years, threw a blazing fastball that often exceeded 100 miles per hour his entire career. He pitched seven no hitters—his last at age 43. Ryan had 5,714 strikeouts—the Major League leader. His career record is 324–292.

Ryan had his number retired by three teams: the Los Angeles Angels, the Houston Astros, and the Texas Rangers. Early in his career, he played for the New York Mets in their 1969 World Series championship season. Ryan is the all-time leader in no-hitters with seven, three more than any other pitcher. He has 12 one-hitters, and 18 two-hitters. Ryan is one of only 29 players in baseball history to have appeared in Major League Baseball games in four different decades. He was inducted into the National Baseball Hall of Fame in 1999.

Santo, Ron

Ron Santo played 14 years for the Chicago Cubs and one for the Chicago White Sox. He was an excellent third baseman. Not always as quick as some infielders, he often dove at the ball and stopped most everything headed down the line. He had a powerful arm and was a tough hitter.

Santo started playing for the Cubs in 1960. The Cubs of the 1960s were a poor team, but they improved as they aged. The Chicago Cubs had fallen on hard times and had not won a World Series since 1908. By the time the 1969 season was midway through, everything was coming together. The team had a roster of stars that included future Hall of Famers Ernie Banks, Ferguson Jenkins, and Billy Williams along with a number of other excellent players such as Glenn Beckert and Don Kessinger. Watching the team's progress was thrilling in July, but by the time September rolled around, for some inexplicable reason, the team was fading fast. When the season ended, the Cubs were in second place in the NL East. It didn't get much better.

Within a few years, the Cubs were back towards the bottom of the NL East. They stayed there for another decade. In 1974, Santo was traded to the White Sox where he spent one season and then retired.

Santo won five straight Gold Glove Awards. He was an All-Star nine times. He led the NL in walks four times. He led the league in on-base percentage two times. Santo retired with a .277 career average, 342 home runs, 1,331 RBIs, 1,108 walks and 1,138 runs scored. Santo led the NL third basemen in putouts seven times and assists seven times. When he retired he held several defensive records for NL third baseman.

Santo returned to the Cubs in 1990 as a radio broadcaster. The great third baseman was inducted into the National Baseball Hall of Fame in 2012.

Scherzer, Max

Max Scherzer has pitched for the Arizona Diamondbacks, the Detroit Tigers, and the Washington Nationals. A power pitcher, he has three Cy Young Awards and pitched two no-hitters. Scherzer is a three time winner of the Sporting News Starting Pitcher of the Year, the first in wins in his league four times, strikeout leader for each nine innings pitched for three seasons, overall strikeout leader for three seasons, and complete game leader for three seasons in the NL.

Scherzer's most memorable game was on June 15, 2015. It was a hot day in Nationals Park in Washington, DC. Scherzer had a perfect game going into the 9th against the Pittsburgh Pirates. With two outs, José Tabata was at the plate with two strikes. On Scherzer's

103rd pitch of the game, he came inside on Tabata with a slider. The ball dinged Tabatha's left elbow protector. Home-plate umpire Mike Muchlinski sent Tabata to first, breaking up the perfect game. Scherzer said the pitch was a slider that he didn't finish and it didn't break much.

A loss of concentration on Scherzer's part might have lost his no-hitter as well. Next up was Josh Harrison. But Scherzer maintained his composure and Harrison flied out to deep left to end the game and give Scherzer the no-hitter. Scherzer pitched for 5 wins and 4 losses in the shortened 2020 season.

Spahn, Warren

"Spahnnie" started his sensational baseball career in 1942 with the Boston Braves at age 21. But with the urgency of World War II, he enlisted in the U.S. Army, serving 3 years. Near the War's end, he served with distinction under General George Patton at the "Battle of the Bulge." After discharge following the end of the War, he resumed his Braves career which lasted 19 seasons—seven in Boston and 12 in Milwaukee where the Braves moved in 1953. He did not win his first Major League game until he was age 25. But for the following two decades he was the most successful left-handed pitcher in the Major League, winning 363 games, the most ever by a left handed pitcher. He won 20 games or more in a season, a record-tying 13 times; pitched two no-hitters; and led the National League in strikeouts 4 consecutive years. He became a master at changing speeds and location to keep hitters off balance. He also had an outstanding pick-off move to first base. He often helped his own cause at the plate hitting 35 home runs over his career. Even at the age of

42, he pitched 22 complete games winning 23 games and losing only seven. Spahn was once asked if he was ever nervous on the pitching mound. He responded, "Nervous? Nervous is during a battle in war when the opposition is shooting rifles with live ammunition meaning to hit you." Spahn was inducted into the National Baseball Hall of Fame in 1973, his first year of eligibility.

Spalding, Albert

Albert Spalding was an early pioneer of baseball. After youth baseball, Spalding joined an amateur team in Rockford, Illinois. From Rockford, he joined up with the Cincinnati Red Stockings where he became known as one of the best pitchers in the game. Spalding signed on with the White Stockings (later named the Chicago Cubs) and worked with owner William Hulbert to create a new National League by recruiting players and teams. For the White Stockings, Spalding pitched/managed for the team and then he served in the front office. With his brother, Spalding created the company A. G. Spalding & Bros. that manufactured and distributed sporting goods. Spalding also advanced the use of the baseball glove, published popular baseball rule books, and organized the first international tour of baseball players. Spalding was inducted into the National Baseball Hall of Fame in 1939.

Suzuki, Ichiro

Suzuki began his MLB career at age 27 in 2001. He would play 19 years in the big leagues. In 2001, he was the AL Rookie of the Year and the AL MVP. He won the AL batting title in 2001 and 2004. He was a 10-time All-Star and an All-Star MVP in 2007. Suzuki was also a Gold

Glove winner 10-times. He stole 56 bases in 2001, the leader for that year. Suzuki's 262 hits in 2004 broke Hall of Fame first baseman George Sisler's record that had been in place for 80 years.

Trout, Mike

Mike Trout, the talented centerfielder for the Los Angeles Angels, is perhaps the greatest baseball player in the game today. Trout is big, strong, and lightning fast. His *accolades*: American League Rookie of the Year in 2012; the Sporting News American League Player of the Year; two-time Henry Aaron Award for Best Hitter in the American League; Wilson Defensive Player of the Year in 2012 for an American League outfielder and the overall Defensive Player of the Year as well; three-time AL MVP; two time All-Star AL MVP; and eight-time AL All-Star.

On May 21, 2013, against the Seattle Mariners, the 21-year-old Trout became the youngest player in the American League to hit for the "cycle"—single, double, triple, and home run in one game. He had to hit a low pitch for the homer in the eighth inning to accomplish it. Trout is fast on the base path. He also throws out runners trying to advance too far on balls hit to his outfield position. And he has made spectacular catches at the wall to rob competitors of home runs.

Trout topped the AL in on-base percentage for four seasons. He was on top of the AL in slugging percentage for three seasons. His career batting average is .304. He has ranked in the AL top ten for home runs five seasons, RBIs four seasons, and bases on balls eight seasons. One of today's best paid players is Mike Trout. Trout banked 17 home runs, 46 RBIs, and a .281 average in the shortened 2020 season.

Vance, Dazzy

Dazzy Vance's story is one of fortitude. He showed great promise as a young player, but he had arm trouble that kept him back to mostly Minor League play from 1915-1921. In 1920, a doctor diagnosed the problem and treated it successfully so that Vance was able to return to the game pain-free. Returning to the big leagues in 1922, Vance was essentially a 31-year old rookie. Vance went on to a Hall of Fame career that lasted through 1935. He was the National League MVP in 1924 when his record was 28–6 for the Brooklyn Robins.

Vance twice led the league in wins in 1924 and 1925. He had the lowest ERA for three seasons, the most shutouts for three seasons, and the most strikeouts for seven seasons. His career win-loss record was 197-140. He was inducted into the National Baseball Hall of Fame in 1955.

Verlander, Justin

Outstanding Justin Verlander is an eight-time MLB All-Star who began his career in Detroit and pitched over 12 seasons for the Tigers. In a trade late in the 2017 season, he came over to the Houston Astros. In Detroit, Verlander was part of four consecutive American League Central Division Championships and two pennants. He was named the 2006 American League Rookie of the Year. Two Cy Young Awards (2011 and 2019) and the Triple Crown for Pitchers in 2011 are among his accomplishments.

He was named the American League MVP in 2011; the Willie Mays World Series MVP Award in 2017; the Sporting News Player of the Year in 2011; the Sporting

Justin Verlander

News Pitcher of the Year in 2011 and 2012 (co-winner); the AL pitching title in 2011; and the 2019 All MLB Team. He was co-winner of the Babe Ruth Award in 2017 for the best performance in the postseason when the Astros won the World Series. In 2018, Verlander earned 200 career wins. He threw three career no-hitters and struck out his 3,000th batter. Verlander has led the AL in strikeouts five times, and in wins twice.

Verlander is the sixth player in Major League history to throw at least three no-hitters. He is in good company, joining Nolan Ryan, Sandy Koufax, Bob Feller, Larry Corcoran, and Cy Young. In the shortened 2020 season, Verlander was injured and underwent ulnar collateral reconstructive (Tommy John) surgery on his right elbow.

Wagner, Honus

Honus Wagner was nicknamed "*The Flying Dutchman.*" Wagner played 21 seasons in the Major League and he was one of the best players. His first three seasons were with the Louisville Cardinals. A native of the Pittsburgh area, he happily played 18 seasons for the Pirates from 1900-1917. Wagner was remarkably versatile; he played shortstop, but he also played every position except for catcher! Wagner was a sturdy 5-foot-11 ballplayer who was bowlegged with huge hands and feet.

A .300-or-better hitter for 15-straight seasons, Wagner won eight National League batting titles. He led the NL in doubles seven times, triples three times, stolen bases five times, RBI four times, slugging percentage six times, and on-base percentage four times.

In Wagner's career, he had 3,420 hits, 643 doubles, 1,739 runs, 1,732 RBIs and 723 stolen bases. He also had a career .328 batting average. Wagner hit with a bat that exceeded 40 ounces and the grip he used had his hands inches apart.

A baseball card was printed up with Wagner's image on it, but it was sold with cigarettes. Because Wagner thought the card would help sell young people on tobacco products, he had the card taken out of circulation and printing ceased. The short supply of the cards have heightened its value to the point where the few cards remaining sell for record-breaking amounts. Wagner was among the first five players inducted into the National Baseball Hall of Fame in 1936.

Walsh, Ed

Ed Walsh was a professional baseball pitcher who played 14 years from 1904–1917—almost entirely for the Chicago White Sox. "Big Ed's" father emigrated from Ireland and his mother from Wales. His parents had 13 children and he began working in the mines at 12 years old. Like many of the early baseball players, Walsh grew up tough and hard.

When Walsh made it to the Major League with the Chicago White Sox, he liked to pitch frequently and often worked long and hard. He overworked his arm causing him to become much less effective in his later career.

Highly competitive by nature, Walsh put much effort into his fielding. He also loved to pick off runners when they managed to get on base. Walsh was a *spitball pitcher* who had a lifetime ERA of 1.82, the lowest of all time. He also pitched a 40-win season for the White Sox in 1908—the last pitcher to do so. He was the last pitcher to pitch 400 innings (also in 1908). He pitched a no-hitter in 1911. Walsh's career record is 195–126. He was inducted into the National Baseball Hall of Fame in 1946.

Williams, Ted

One of the greatest hitters of all time was Ted Williams. Williams got on base almost half the time he entered the batter's box. The "Splendid Splinter's" lifetime on-base average was .482. Williams believed in hitting for a combination of average and power. Williams was the last Major League Baseball player to have hit for over .400 for a season.

Born in San Diego in 1918, Williams father was a photographer and his mother was a devoted Salvation Army evangelist who was Mexican-American. His future as one of the greatest hitters was predictable by his endless practice and focus from an early age at hitting. Williams would hit and hit and hit baseballs. Disciplined and competitive, he knew the strike zone perfectly. He seldom swung at pitches outside of it.

Williams was a professional baseball outfielder for the Boston Red Sox who played from 1939–1960 with breaks for military service. He served as a pilot in World War II and the Korean War. In his 19-year career, he was an All-Star for 17 seasons. Williams was the American League Most Valuable Player for two seasons and the American League batting champion for six seasons. He won the *Triple Crown* for two seasons. Williams retired with a career .344 batting average and 521 home runs. He was inducted into the Hall of Fame in 1966.

Williams was always interested in learning more on baseball. He often talked with great hitters and pitchers. He conveyed that knowledge in *The Science of Hitting* that he wrote with journalist John Underwood. In his book, Williams talks about how important dedication is to the process.

Williams displayed dedication, determination, athleticism, and endless effort. He wanted to be remembered as the "best hitter that ever lived."

Wilson, Hack

At 5-foot-6 and 190 pounds, "Hack" Wilson played in Major League Baseball for 12 seasons. Beginning with the New York Giants late in 1923, Wilson helped the Giants win the pennant in 1924 by hitting .295. The Chicago Cubs signed Wilson in 1926.

Wilson had been raised in difficult conditions. Cubs manager at the time, Joe McCarthy, took special care with Wilson and his performance reflected their respect for each other. With the Cubs, he led the NL in home runs four times and RBIs twice. Wilson was a solid centerfielder who led the league in fielding percentage in 1926 and putouts in 1927. Wilson led the NL with 159 RBIs in 1929 while fueling the Cubs to the NL Pennant. In 1930, Wilson's NL record-breaking 56 home runs stood for 68 years. His 191 RBIs in 1930 is a Major League single-season record that some believe will never be broken. He capped off the season with a .356 batting average.

Wilson played for the Brooklyn Dodgers for three seasons after the Cubs and finished up with a few games for the Philadelphia Phillies.

Wilson drove in more than 100 runs in six of his 12 seasons. He ended his career with a lifetime .307 average, 244 home runs and 1,063 RBIs. He also led the league in walks twice and retired with a .395 on-base percentage. Wilson was inducted into the National Baseball Hall of Fame in 1979.

Wright, Harry

Considered by many to be the founder of professional baseball, Harry Wright put together the first professional team. He managed and played outfield for the 1869 Cincinnati Red Stockings. Once the Cincinnati team was disbanded, Wright managed teams in Boston, Providence and Philadelphia with 1,225 victories and six pennants. Wright was inducted into the National Baseball Hall of Fame in 1953.

Born in England, the son of a Cricket player, Wright promoted baseball as a new sport and he was heavily involved in all aspects of the game in the second half of the 19th century.

Yelich, Christian

Christian Yelich is an outfielder for the Milwaukee Brewers who is one of the best hitters in the game. Coming over from the Miami Marlins in the 2018 preseason, Yelich notched over 30 home runs, 20 stolen bases, and a batting average over .325 for both his first two Brewer seasons. The 6-foot-3 28 year old won the 2018 and 2019 National League batting titles, the 2018 National League MVP Award, and the 2018 and 2019 Hank Aaron Award.

Yelich hit for the cycle—single, double, triple, and home run—twice in 2018. Yelich's performance suffered in the shortened 2020 season.

Christian Yelich

Young, Cy

The Cy Young Award is given each year to the best pitcher in the American and in the National leagues. The Baseball Writers' Association of America (BBWAA) votes on the award at the conclusion of each season. Baseball's most prestigious pitching award was named after Cy Young, the 6-foot-2 pitcher who played from 1890–1911. Young was one of the early pitchers who worked through the change in pitching distance. Between the 1892 and 1893 seasons, the distance between the pitcher and batter was increased from 55 feet 6 inches to 60 feet 6 inches.

Young first played for the Cleveland Spiders. In 1892 for the Spiders, he was 36–12 with an ERA of 1.93. He played for the Saint Louis Perfectos/Cardinals in 1899–1900. In Saint Louis in 1899, he was 26–16 with 40 complete games! He went on to play for the Boston Americans/Red Sox 1901–1908. In Boston in 1901, he was 33–10 with an ERA of 1.62. He played over 2 years with the Cleveland Naps and finished out 1911 with the Boston Rustlers.

Young's 511 career wins and his 7,356 innings pitched are records that may never get beat. Young had 16 seasons of 20 or more wins and five seasons of 30 or more wins. He ended his career with three no-hitters including one perfect game.

Young had his own methods. He wanted to save his arm for games so he did not pitch much in training camp. During the season, he took few practice pitches. He also thought that allowing a hitter to ground out or pop out was much preferred to a strikeout because it could be done with far fewer pitches. His methods allowed him to pitch every other day when needed. Cy Young was inducted into the National Baseball Hall of Fame in 1937.

Cy Young

Origins and Early History

Who played the first game of baseball? It is a riddle that only the *Sphinx* can solve. Some trace it all the way back to ancient Egypt! Most insist that baseball is truly an American game although it developed from an old game called *Rounders* and perhaps older games still.

Rounders is an English schoolboy game which can be traced back as far as the *Elizabethan Era* in England. A poem which exclaims the joy of such a game was mentioned in John Newbery's 1744 *Little Pretty Pocket Book*.

Base Ball

The ball once struck off,
Away flies the boy
To the next destin'd post,
And then how with Joy.

Rounders in America was called "town ball." Played at the time of "town meetings." Imagine parents inside the town hall debating the issues of the town—young people outside playing ball.

In New England the game was referred to as the "Boston game" or the "Massachusetts game." It was often played on *Boston Common* during the 1830s. The number of players on a side might vary. The field was an irregular *polygon* with five bases including home base and a batter's box. It was a short distance to first base, but an extra-long distance to second base. The ball was made of any soft and elastic material. The pitcher threw underhanded. He was known as the "thrower," "feeder," or "giver." His function was to pitch the ball where the batter could hit it. The batter could even request the kind of pitch he wanted to hit, such as high or low, inside or outside. He stood inside the polygon towards the center. A catcher stood close behind the hitter to catch any misses or bad pitches, but he also had a fielder or "scout" behind him to assist him if he missed it.

Outs were made when hit balls were caught on the fly or on one bounce. Runners were called out if a scout or fielder hit them with the ball on the base path. The preferred technique for this was for a scout to get as close to a runner as possible and then whip the ball as hard as he could at him so as not to miss him. The hitter got as many swings as he needed to hit the ball.

In the 1840s, the "modern game" was born in New York. Some suggest that the birth of baseball was a mutation—an unexpected change in the evolution of bat and ball games. Some historians have reported that in 1842 in a playfield in New York, a young man named Alexander J. Cartwright diagrammed a new layout for the game using a diamond to mark the field. The field came to feature an iron plate for home base and three bases. Rounders typically used posts for these.

A defensive fielder was assigned to each base and three more fielders in the outfield. Add a "feeder" to toss an underhand pitch. Add a catcher behind the hitter to handle the pitched ball and baseball was born! There were originally eight players to a side. Later an extra fielder was added that eventually became what we know today as a shortstop.

This became known as the "New York" game. People still debate about whether Cartwright should get credit for all these innovations.

But a group of young men from the New York City Knickerbocker Club were so excited by Cartwright's baseball and new rules that they formed a team to play it. An organizational meeting was held on September 23, 1845 for that purpose. Soon a challenge was issued by another New York athletic association. Rules were agreed upon between the teams based on the New York game. The first "official" game of baseball was held the following year on June 19, 1846, at the Elysian Fields in Hoboken, New Jersey. Cartwright, also a surveyor, supervised the laying out of the field, explained the rules, and served as the game's umpire.

When news of the Knickerbockers' new game traveled to Boston, their game took root with a Boston club. Soon more and more teams were playing the New York game.

Later, during the Civil War, baseball was played by both union and confederate armies to pass time between battles, making it truly an "American" game. On occasion, a game was stopped to allow the soldiers to run to the firing line! Baseball was even played by soldiers *incarcerated* in prison camps who taught it to their captors! When the war ended, thousands of soldiers on both sides spread the game upon returning home.

At first, players were unpaid amateurs. But by 1869 a team in Cincinnati recruited the best players and began to pay them to play. This proved to be a very successful idea. The Cincinnati "Red Stockings" became the first professional team. Taking on all comers and touring the country, the Red Stockings won 138 straight contests until finally losing to a team from Brooklyn, New York, in extra innings. The Red Stockings broke up as a team, but its success sparked the emergence of other professional teams.

The team manager, *Harry Wright*, moved to Boston where he started a new team, recruiting emerging pitching star *Albert Spalding* from Rockford, Illinois. Spalding later returned to Chicago to start another new team, the Chicago White Stockings, that later became the Chicago Cubs.

By 1876 a league of the top teams formed what is now known as, the National League. The stage was set for huge developments in the 20th century.

20th Century Story of Baseball and America

Once the game was established, it continued to develop and became our national pastime. And regardless of the hardships Americans experienced, baseball carried on and the players entertained fans.

Early 20th Century

In terms of American history, the 20th century began on rocky ground. President William McKinley was assassinated in 1901. Theodore Roosevelt took over as 26th president of the United States. Roosevelt was one of our most energetic presidents. He would serve in the Oval Office until March 1909.

Baseball was an established game by the start of the 20th century. Baseball success grew and the National League, which had begun in 1876, was being challenged by the new American League that had begun Major League status play in 1901.

By 1903, the National League and the American League agreed to have their champions meet in a series of games at the end of the season that became the first World Series. The number of games it took to win the series would change in the early years.

Great players entertained fans. Honus Wagner, the league's leading hitter, batted .352 for the first decade. Veteran pitcher Cy Young won an average of 28 games a season with a 2.14 ERA for the first 5 years. Tiny Wee

Willy Keeler regularly ran out infield hits, bunted safely, stole bases in bunches, and drove balls to open spaces.

In that first World Series, pitcher Bill Dinneen of the Boston Americans won Game 8 (in a best-of-nine-game series) against the highly touted Pittsburgh Pirates. Dinneen would strike out Honus Wagner for the final out.

The National League New York Giants led by Manager John McGraw would win the NL Championship in 1904. But McGraw stubbornly refused to play the American League Champions, the Boston Americans, because he considered the league inferior. Many disagreed and McGraw decided to "*play ball*" the following year. The series resumed in 1905 when the Giants beat the Philadelphia Athletics. The series would continue annually each year except in 1994 when it was cancelled due to a players' strike. In the first decade (1900-1909), the Chicago Cubs would play in the series three times, losing one to the Chicago White Sox in 1906 then beating the Detroit Tigers in both 1907 and 1908. The championship in 1908 would be the last one won by the Cubs in over 100 years! The next Cubs' World Series win would be in 2016.

Manager Connie Mack's Philadelphia Athletics beat the Cubs in a best-of-seven World Series in 1910—they'd win again in 1913 against the Giants. In 1911, Ty Cobb batted .419 for the season. "Shoeless" Joe Jackson trailed at .408. Cobb also led the league in hits, runs, doubles, triples, stolen bases, slugging, and runs batted in.

In 1916, Babe Ruth was pitching for the Boston Red Sox. His record was 23–12 for the season. In 1918, Ruth won two games in the World Series against the Cubs. Boston would take the series, four games to two.

In 1919, the Chicago White Sox faced the Cincinnati Reds in the World Series. The Sox lost the best-of-nine game series, five games to three. Rumors surfaced that Sox players were bribed by gamblers to lose games in the series. Known as the "1919 Black Sox Scandal," it was established that eight of the heavily-favored Chicago White Sox had either participated or knew about the plot. New Baseball Commissioner, Kenesaw Mountain Landis, a former federal judge, decided to ban those players for life from playing baseball.

When fans lose confidence in a sport due to dishonest play it can have a long-lasting effect. Luckily for baseball, Babe Ruth started belting out home runs in the next decade attracting fans to the games in large numbers.

World War I

On June 28, 1914, a Yugoslav nationalist Gavrilo Princip assassinated the Austro-Hungarian Empire's Archduke Franz Ferdinand. The assassination led to war between Austria-Hungary and Serbia. Soon many European countries entered the conflict because of alliances that tied them together. The war became the first global conflict or World War.

Nationalism, the belief that people of the same ethnic type, language, and political ideas should be allowed to form their own governments was one cause of conflicts. Imperialism, the policy and effort to expand by diplomacy or force one country's power and control into foreign markets was another cause of hostilities. As tensions increased in part from growing nationalism and imperialism, countries expanded their military operations.

Nations that formed the Allied powers (United Kingdon, France, Russia, Italy, United States, and others) fought the Central powers (Germany, Austria-

Hungary, Turkey, Bulgaria). Factors such as the escalation of German submarine attacks on U.S. merchant vessels led the U.S. Congress to declare war on Germany on April 6, 1917.

World War I was especially brutal. It lasted in Europe from 1914-1918. It involved many countries and included an especially horrific type of fighting called trench warfare. In trench warfare, both sides dug trenches to protect themselves at the *battlefront* from *artillery* and machine guns. When soldiers left the trenches to charge the enemy, many were killed and wounded. Poison gas was also used in World War I. At first, the types used were meant to be a temporary irritant. More harmful varieties were used in time. Long after the war, soldiers suffered from ailments caused by it. About 8-10 million men died and another 20 million were wounded during World War I.

Many professional ballplayers, like stars Ty Cobb and Eddie Collins, patriotically joined the military to serve the country in the war effort. The recently retired pitching star, Christy Mathewson, also enlisted. "Matty" served in the United States Army's Chemical Warfare Service where he was accidentally exposed to chemical weapons during training. This exposure to poison chemical gas is thought to have led to his contracting tuberculosis from which he died.

Power of Ruth

Babe Ruth was a sensation. Before he became known as a hitter, he was a pitcher. Pitchers need to focus most of their time on pitching. In normal circumstances, they play fewer games than a fielder. The Red Sox saw that the Babe could hit so they tried to use him in several ways. In 1919, the Red Sox had Ruth pitching, playing the outfield and first base. He hit 29 home runs—a record at the time.

The Red Sox owner, Harry Frazee, invested money in Broadway plays and the Boston Red Sox. Frazee sold Ruth's services to the New York Yankees after the 1919 season. Some sources blame Frazee for selling a super star, but others suggest he had good reasons.

CURVEBALL QUIZ

Who managed the "A"s for 50 years?

ANSWER ON FOLLOWING PAGE

[Curveball Quiz Solution: Connie Mack.]

Goodbye to the Dead ball Era

Once the Yankees had Ruth, they experimented with different field assignments, but he was in the lineup every day and hitting more home runs than anyone thought was possible. The 1920 Yankees were the first Major League Baseball team to have more than one million fans in attendance with Ruth hitting an incredible 54 home runs.

Ruth's enthusiasm came through in stories and interviews. The public couldn't get enough of the Babe. He said things from the heart. He visited sick kids and signed balls for them. New York especially loved the Babe. In 1923, Yankee Stadium opened to a crowd of 74,217 with a 4–1 win over the Red Sox featuring a Ruth homer. That season the Yankees would also win their first World Series. Another big Yankee slugger, Lou Gehrig, was a rookie that year.

In the 1920s, seven World Series featured the New York Yankees managed by Miller Huggins, the New York Giants managed by John McGraw, or both teams playing each other!

The St. Louis Cardinals came out of the pack in the National League to win the pennant in 1926. With future Hall of Famer Rogers Hornsby as manager and second baseman, the Cardinals defeated the Yanks in the World Series. In Game 7, the Cardinals notched the final out throwing Ruth out at second attempting to steal.

Great Depression

With the Stock Market Crash of 1929, the Great Depression took hold of the country and much of the world for over a decade. Many people lost everything they had. Poverty was the new normal.

Former President Teddy Roosevelt's distant cousin, Franklin Delano Roosevelt (FDR), became president during the Great Depression on March 4, 1933. FDR gave talks on the radio that were meant to assure Americans that things would get better. These talks were called "Fireside Chats." Roosevelt was determined to do everything he could to project a positive attitude and encourage Americans during the tough times. In Washington, he was sometimes seen at the baseball stadium. In 1937, FDR tossed out the first pitch on opening day at Griffith Stadium where the Washington Senators defeated the Philadelphia Athletics.

Franklin Delano Roosevelt introduced many programs in what was called his New Deal. In order to help the country pull out of the Depression, he focused on what was called the 3-Rs: relief, recovery, and reform. These programs helped give the country some direction and hope.

Baseball Wins America's Heart

With radio coverage, cheap tickets, and newspaper coverage, Major League Baseball carried on. The World Series champions for 1929 and 1930 were the Philadelphia Athletics—a team that had often been in the hunt for championships. But after 1930, the A's would not see another World Series for 42 years and it would be as the Oakland Athletics.

One of the big stars of the 1930s was first baseman and outfielder Hank Greenberg who played for Detroit. The Tigers had been down in the standings for several years. In the mid-thirties, Greenberg and three other future Hall of Famers were on the Tigers' roster: catcher

Mickey Cochrane, second baseman Charlie Gehringer, and leftfielder Goose Goslin. In 1934 and 1935, Greenberg's Tigers won the pennant.

In 1934, the Tigers lost the series to the Cardinals who were called the "Gas House Gang." The Gas House Gang was a gritty team that featured the pitching duo of brothers Dizzy and Paul Dean. The Brothers Dean won all four games of the 1934 series for the Cardinals.

For the *Motor City* (Detroit), the 1935 series was a different story. The Tigers beat the Chicago Cubs in six games. It would be the Tigers first World Series win. Detroit, the fourth largest city in the United States at the time, celebrated the victory into the early morning hours.

In 1938, Greenberg hit 58 home runs, just shy of Ruth's record of 60. Greenberg would play for 13 years and tally 331 home runs. Like many players of the time, his baseball career would be interrupted by military service. Greenberg was in the U.S. Army Air Force from 1942-1944.

Under a new coach, Joe McCarthy, the Yankees closed out the 1930s with three straight World Series championships. Ruth's last season with the Yankees was in 1934, but a new superstar was emerging in the outfield for the Yankees, Joe DiMaggio.

Surviving the War Years

The Cincinnati Reds played the Detroit Tigers in the 1940 World Series. The Reds won the series in seven games with a 2–1 squeaker to close.

Notable on the Reds roster was future Hall of Fame catcher, Ernie Lombardi, and pitcher Johnny Vander Meer. In 1938, a young Vander Meer threw two-consecutive no-hitters in June. Hats off to Vander Meer for his great back-to-back performances, but credit also goes to Lombardi. Lombardi excelled at *calling the game* for pitchers.

War was looming over America as the 1940s began. Events in Europe had Americans' attention, but the big story here was Joe DiMaggio's 56-game hitting streak in 1941. Unlike Ruth, DiMaggio was a quiet and private person, but by the time the season ended, every American knew who Joe DiMaggio was and what he accomplished.

As DiMaggio passed other hitting streak records such as Ty Cobb's 40-game streak or Wee Willy Keeler's all-time consecutive streak of 44 games, the pressure mounted. Fans woke up each day to read about DiMaggio's performance from the previous day in the newspaper. Many listened to the radio to catch the action live on days that the Yankees played. The streak was a continuous story that ran until DiMaggio went hitless on July 17, 1941.

The Yankees were back in the championship chase and beat the Dodgers in the 1941 series. The Yankees lost to the Cardinals in the 1942 series and then beat the Cardinals in the 1943 series. The Yankees would beat the Dodgers in 1947 and 1949. The "Bronx Bombers" were definitely the class of Major League Baseball in the 1940s with five series appearances and four Victories.

The Cardinals would appear in four World Series in the 1940s: 1942, 1943, 1944, and 1946.

The Cardinals were formidable. It was the early days for the Cards' Stan "the Man" Musial, one of the greatest players in the history of the game. In 1943, Musial was the NL MVP. In 1942, Cardinals pitcher Matt Cooper won the NL MVP. In 1942 and 1946, the Cardinals also had future Hall of Famer Enos "Country" Slaughter who would serve in the military from 1943-1945.

World War II

About a dozen years after the beginning of the Great Depression and a few months after DiMaggio's hitting streak, the United States entered World War II as a combatant with the bombing of *Pearl Harbor* on December 7, 1941. The origins of the conflict were much older.

Ending World War I was the Treaty of Versailles that contributed to almost impossible post-war conditions in Germany that helped fuel power struggles between the government and other political groups. Groups supporting radical dictatorship and nationalism came to power in Germany, Italy, and Japan. These countries formed the Axis powers. They expanded their boundaries by force.

The war itself began in Europe with the German invasion of Poland in 1939. Poland was part of the Allies alliance, which included France and the United Kingdom. The alliance expanded as the War evolved into a global conflict. Russia signed a non-aggression pact with Germany in 1939, but found itself under attack by Germany in 1941.

When the Japanese attacked Pearl Harbor, the United States declared War on Japan on December 8, 1941. Germany and Italy joined the conflict against the United States on the side of Japan on December 11. Germany especially committed atrocities during the period when Adolf Hitler was the Furor or leader of Germany.

After the United States entered the war, American forces were mobilized. A great number of men entered the military. Many professional baseball players joined the military or were drafted, such as future stars Yogi Berra and Warren Spahn. President Franklin

Roosevelt would continue to serve as president until his death on April 12, 1945, towards the end of the war. Vice President *Harry Truman* would take over as president at that time. The impact of both World War I and World War II can still be seen throughout portions of the world.

Fabulous 50s

Managing the Boston Red Sox in 1948, Joe McCarthy's team lost a one-game playoff for the American League pennant to Cleveland. In 1949, the Red Sox lost the pennant on the last day of the season. McCarthy, the winningest manager in MLB history, would retire during the 1950 season. Red Sox left fielder, Ted Williams, would remain in Boston throughout the decade. Williams would be a 19-time All-Star; he would be the AL Most Valuable Player twice; he would be a Triple Crown winner twice; and he would win six batting titles. Williams would play for 19 seasons, but he would only play in one World Series. His Boston Red Sox would lose to the Cardinals in seven games in 1946.

In 1950, Yankees rookie pitcher Whitey Ford had nine wins and only one loss for the season. In the 1950 World Series, the Yankees swept the Philadelphia Phillies four games to none, but each contest was close.

In 1951, the National League Pennant race was the story in baseball. In early August, the New York Giants were 13 1/2 games behind the NL leading Brooklyn Dodgers. At the regular season end, the Giants had tied the Dodgers forcing a best-of-three series for the pennant. In the series, the two teams fought each other *tooth and nail* into the last half of the ninth inning of the third and final game. The Dodgers had the lead, 4–1, with the Giants at bat. With one out, the Giants scored a run. Then, with two men on, slugger Bobby Thompson came up to the plate. With one strike, Thomson hit a line drive that rocketed over left fielder Andy Pafko's head and climbed over the wall to win the game. In a bit of baseball *hyperbole*, the hit became known as "*the shot heard round the world.*"

Managed by Casey Stengel with Joe DiMaggio in his last season and Mickey Mantle in his first, the Yankees proved to be too much for the Giants in the 1951 World Series. The Yankees won in six games.

While the Yankees were thrilling New Yorkers in the 1950s, the exodus of teams out west was underway. The Dodgers would be playing in Los Angeles and the Giants would be playing in San Francisco starting in 1958.

With four future Hall of Famers: pitcher Warren Spahn; second baseman, Red Shoendienst; third baseman Eddie Matthews; and right fielder/third baseman Hank Aaron—the Milwaukee Braves won the pennant in 1957 and 1958. They beat the Yankees in the Series Championship in 1957, but lost the 1958 World Series to the same Yanks.

Korean War

In 1910, Korea was annexed by Japan. It was part of Japan until the Japanese surrendered at the end of World War II (1945). After the war, Korea was split into two parts—one was the Communist state in the North and the other was the Republic in the South. At this time, animosity was building between the United States and Communists in China and the USSR (Soviet Union). The Korean War began on June 25, 1950, when North Korea invaded South Korea from the 38th parallel, the line dividing the two Koreas. The United States and its allies feared that the Soviet Union and

Communist China had encouraged this invasion as a means of increasing communist influence. President Truman committed United States air, ground, and naval forces to the combined United Nations forces assisting the Republic of Korea. World War I and World War II veteran General Douglas MacArthur was put in charge of the United Nations Command.

The North Korean forces advanced and pushed the forces of the South towards the southern end of the peninsula. General MacArthur surprised the North Koreans with a daring amphibious landing behind North Korean lines. Then the United Nations forces pushed the North Koreans all the way to the Chinese border. At that point, the Chinese army directly entered the conflict with a huge army and drove the UN forces to the south and seized the South Korean capital of Seoul.

In early 1951, the United Nations Command, strengthened by the 8th U.S. Army led by General Matthew B. Ridgway, retook Seoul and advanced back to the 38th parallel. MacArthur wanted to strike further back at the Chinese, but Truman feared a much larger conflict that would lead to another world-wide war. Truman relieved MacArthur of his command and replaced him with General Ridgway. When Eisenhower followed Truman as president, he was able to end the conflict with an armistice signed on July 27, 1953, that leaves Korea split in two, much as had been at the end of World War II at the 38th parallel. The Korean peninsula continues to be an area of concern.

Many MLB players served during the Korean War, assisting in the effort to prevent North Korea from imposing communist rule on South Korea. One of those was Ted Williams. Williams originally enlisted during World War II. After 2 years of training, he obtained a commission in the Marine Corps and served until 1946 in the Reserve Aviation Unit as an instructor. He was called back to the military during the Korean War. He flew with the Third Marine Air Wing, 223rd Squadron, and his plane was hit multiple times. On one mission, his plane was damaged so badly, he had to crash land it, but Williams was airborne again the following day. Williams flew 39 missions.

Cold War Crisis

The Cold War was a period of tension primarily between the Soviet Union and the United States and their allies after World War II. The period spans from the 1947 *Truman Doctrine* to the 1991 dissolution of the Soviet Union. The Korean War and the war in Vietnam had origins that were older than the Cold War, but they were both conflicts that were affected by it. Other key events helped define the Cold War.

Truman Doctrine

Before World War II, the Western democracies faced threats from Communism and Fascism. Fascism was beaten back, but Communism continued to grow after the war. Russia used its occupation of countries in Eastern Europe to expand its brand of Communism.

In Greece, the cradle of democracy, the German occupation during World War II had destroyed the country's infrastructure. This caused much suffering and political instability that promoted communism. Similar conditions were present in Turkey. President Truman announced an aid package to Greece and Turkey on March 12, 1947, that would help the countries recover. Congress passed legislation to provide it. In Truman's speech, he offered a strategy that would become known as the Truman Doctrine of containment. The Truman

Doctrine was used to support the alliance of Western European nations in other situations. The North Atlantic Treaty Organization (NATO) that banded together western nations for their mutual aid and defense was created in 1949 as a means of containment.

The Truman Doctrine was later invoked to oppose aggression in Germany from Communist Russia, and later in the mid-1950s to contain aggression in South Korea from Communist China. Many historians label the Truman Doctrine as the beginning of the "Cold War." Its influence lasted forty years until the fall of the Berlin Wall and the collapse of Communist Soviet Union. When the Berlin Wall finally crumbled, a reunified Germany became prosperous and free to choose its political leaders in democratic elections.

Berlin Airlift, 1948-1949

At the end of the Second World War, the United States, France, the United Kingdom, and the Soviet Union occupied Germany. Led by Secretary of State George Marshall and funded by Congress, the Marshall Plan was established to provide aid for Western Europe to revitalize the nations suffering the effects of the War.

The United States, France, and the United Kingdom were in West Germany and the Soviet Union was in East Germany. Although the important city of Berlin was in the East, the western portion of the city was controlled by the United States, France, and the United Kingdom. A supply line from the west was routed through Soviet-controlled East Germany to West Berlin.

As the relationship between the Western Allies and the Soviet Union became hostile, on June 24, 1948, Soviet forces blockaded rail, road, and water access to Allied-controlled areas of Berlin. In response, the United

States and the United Kingdom began the enormous job of airlifting food and fuel to Berlin. The West's resolve to help the Germans never wavered. The crisis ended on May 12, 1949, when Soviet forces lifted the blockade on land access to western Berlin.

U-2 Spy Plane

The Cold War lasted several decades. In May 1960, Francis Gary Powers was piloting a U-2 "Spy Plane" on a reconnaissance mission for the *Central Intelligence Agency (CIA)*. A poison pin concealed in a silver dollar was taken along on the flight. Powers was thirteen hundred miles inside of Russia when he started flying the plane manually. After several hours of flying, a Soviet surface-to-air missile aimed at his plane exploded behind the craft damaging the U-2, which began spiraling out of control. Powers managed to climb out of his plane. His parachute opened and he started to sail down to earth. He saw a piece of his plane float down past him. Powers considered using the poison pin, but he decided not to lose hope of escape. Realizing the silver dollar would most likely be confiscated, he removed the pin and placed it in his pocket. He tossed the coin into the field below.

On Powers' flight down, he saw men trailing him in a vehicle. Upon landing, Powers was arrested, taken to the Moscow headquarters of the KGB (security agency of the Soviet Union), and interrogated for several weeks.

Powers was tried for espionage and sentenced to ten years of confinement at Vladimir Prison. On February 10, 1962, Powers was exchanged for Colonel Rudolf Abel, a Soviet spy convicted in the United States of espionage. When Powers got home many people thought he had betrayed his country by not taking the poison pin, but in fact, he had served bravely. Powers was submitted to a public hearing before Congress. He was cleared of all allegations of misconduct. Powers published a memoir of his U-2 experience titled, *Operation Overflight: A Memoir of the U-2 Incident*. His story was also told in the Steven Spielberg-Tom Hanks movie, "Bridge of Spies."

Cuban Missile Crisis

The Cuban Missile Crisis of October 1962 was another Cold War confrontation between the United States and the Soviet Union. Cuba is only 90 miles off Florida. Intelligence sources in the United States led top American officials to believe the leader of Cuba, Fidel Castro, would become another Russian threat to Democracy by leading Cuba and other nations towards Communism. After a failed U.S. attempt to overthrow the Castro regime in Cuba with the *Bay of Pigs* invasion, Soviet Premier Nikita Khrushchev reached a secret agreement with Castro to place Soviet nuclear missiles in Cuba to deter any future invasion attempt. In response to an arms buildup on Cuba and the offensive threat of missiles brought to the West, on September 4, 1962, President Kennedy issued a public warning against the introduction of offensive weapons into Cuba. The next month, U-2 aircraft photographs showed sites for ballistic nuclear missiles under construction in Cuba. On October 22, President Kennedy ordered a naval "quarantine" of Cuba. Kennedy sent a letter to Khrushchev declaring that the United States would not permit offensive weapons to be delivered to Cuba, and demanded that the Soviets dismantle the missile bases and return all offensive weapons to the U.S.S.R.

The President went on national television that evening to inform the public of the developments in Cuba, his decision to initiate and enforce a "quarantine," and the potential global consequences if the crisis continued to escalate: "It shall be the policy of this nation to regard any nuclear missile launched from Cuba against any nation in the Western Hemisphere as an attack by the Soviet Union on the United States, requiring a full retaliatory response upon the Soviet Union." Then, U.S. reconnaissance flights over Cuba indicated the Soviet missile sites were nearing operational readiness—meaning war was on the horizon.

Through a few different channels, messages came in to the President that Russia would dismantle their missile operations if conditions were met. First, the U.S. would agree not to invade Cuba and then a second later condition that the U.S. would pull their missiles from Turkey. After a U.S. spy plane was shot down over Cuba, the crisis heated up again and the United States prepared to invade Cuba. Attorney General Robert Kennedy met with the Soviet Ambassador to the United States, Anatoly Dobrynin, telling him the missiles in Turkey were already scheduled for removal. A short time later the missile sites were taken down in Cuba followed by the end of the "quarantine" and finally removal of missiles from Turkey.

Swinging 1960s

The Yankees were in the first five World Series of the 1960s. They won two and lost three.

The 1960 World Series between the Yankees and the Pirates went down to the seventh game, to the bottom of the ninth. The game was a high scoring affair that the Yankees had just tied up 9–9 in their half of the inning.

Up to bat strolled second baseman Bill Mazerowski for the most important at bat in his 17-season career. The tall thin pitcher for the Yankees, Ralph Terry, tossed his first pitch high, ball one. The second pitch came in down the middle and boom! Mazerowski got every bit of it and sent it over the wall in left. The Pirates won.

After beating the Reds in five games in the 1961 World Series, the Yankees were pennant winners again in 1962. The Yankees played the San Francisco Giants that year and won the series in seven games. Ralph Terry, who had pitched the home run ball to Mazerowski in 1960, was the World Series MVP in 1962.

The Dodgers swept the Yankees in the 1963 series and the Yankees were beaten by the Cardinals in seven in 1964.

The Dodgers returned to the series in 1965 and beat the Twins in seven games. The Dodgers had future Hall of Fame pitchers Sandy Koufax and Don Drysdale. The Dodgers fell behind two games to none, but came back to win the series in seven games.

The Twins had Harmon "Killer" Killebrew. Killebrew was a power hitter who would play for 22 years. He led the league in home runs six times and was a 13-time All-Star. Killebrew frightened pitchers. Often, they tried to "pitch around him." He led the league in walks four times. Killebrew might have been a "Killer" on the field, but those who knew him said he was a wonderful man who often went out of his way to help others. Killebrew hit 573 home runs in his career.

The Baltimore Orioles beat the Dodgers in 1966. It was the St. Louis Cardinals over the Red Sox in 1967. Detroit beat St. Louis in 1968. As the decade was coming to a close in 1969, the Mets beat the Orioles.

Baseball often involves stories of quiet heroes who are revered at home for giving thrills to loyal fans. From

May 12, 1968, to May 18, 1968, the 6-foot-7, 255 pound Washington Senator, Frank Howard, walloped 10 homers in 20 times at bat. Howard was a quiet humble man who was a streaky hitter. When he hit towering home runs, the Senators painted the seats white where some of his biggest hits landed.

Vietnam War

From November 1, 1955, to April 30, 1975, the Vietnam War was waged in Southeast Asia. The twenty year conflict was fought between the Communist government of North Vietnam, who were supported by the Chinese, and the army of South Vietnam, who were supported by the United States of America and others. The conflict's history was long and complicated involving China, France, and others. The collapse of the French Empire in Southeast Asia had led to the existence of North and South Vietnam. Southeast Asia became a powder keg of cold war conflict between Russia, China, and the United States and its allies. The United States favored a policy of containment during the *Cold War*, to prevent Communist aggression. This policy led to an escalation of conflict in the area that continued until the United States withdrew and the Communist forces took control of the entire country.
Americans would become painfully aware of the problems in Vietnam as our soldiers were sent over especially during the 1960s.

Sweet 1970s

The baseball players union gained strength and leverage in the 1970s, sending players' salaries to great heights and allowing for more movement. In this way it was the sweet 1970s for the players.

In 1970, Bud Selig and the Milwaukee Brewers organization purchased the bankrupt Seattle Pilots franchise and quickly moved the team to Milwaukee, Wisconsin. In 1972, the Washington Senators relocated to Arlington, Texas, becoming the Rangers.

Several of the great hitters reached important markers in 1970. The Braves Hank Aaron and the Giants Willie Mays, reached the 3,000 hit pinnacle. Ernie Banks hit his 500th home run. On May 10, Braves knuckleballer Hoyt Wilhelm pitched in his 1,000th game.

The Cincinnati Reds were the "Big Red Machine" and they played in four World Series that decade, winning two. The Orioles beat the Reds in the 1970 World Series with Brooks Robinson awarded MVP. The Oakland A's won three World Series in a row. The Yankees came on strong with two World Series championships late in the decade and the Pirates won one early in 1971 and came back for another in 1979. Reggie Jackson was on teams that won half the World Series in the decade: Oakland A's, 1972-1974 and New York Yankees 1977-1978.

Fast and Furious 1980s

In the 1980s, baseball saw 14 teams in the World Series: Baltimore Orioles, Boston Red Sox, Detroit Tigers, Los Angeles Dodgers, Kansas City Royals, Milwaukee Brewers, Minnesota Twins, New York Mets, New York Yankees, Oakland Athletics, Philadelphia Phillies, San Diego Padres, San Francisco Giants, and St. Louis Cardinals. This was a major development for parity because in the 1970s, only eight teams played in all 10 World Series. In the 1960s, only 11 teams played in the series.

Kirk Gibson was a 17-year veteran of Major League Baseball. Gibson showed great promise. In his early days, he was compared to Mickey Mantle, but his many injuries held him back. Despite his problems, Gibson had a knack for playing well in tough situations. In the 1984 World Series, Detroit was up against the Padres. The Tigers led the series three games to one, but Detroit and Gibson had lived through many disappointments. Every game was crucial, Detroit's last series victory was in 1968.

In Game 5, Gibson came to bat in the eighth inning with one out, Detroit leading, 5–4. Detroit had runners on second and third. San Diego Manager, Future Hall of Famer, Dick Williams, came out to talk with another future Hall of Famer, pitcher Goose Gossage. Gossage was confident he could get Gibson out, so Williams paced back to the dugout.

There was a lot riding on this at-bat. Gibson could add to the Tigers' razor-thin lead or an out could swing the momentum in San Diego's favor. The first pitch was a ball. The tension grew. Gibson dug in and with supreme confidence and concentration slammed the next pitch deep into the right-field bleachers for three runs. Detroit would remember Gibson forever.

In 1988, Gibson had moved out west. He was playing for the Dodgers in World Series Game 1 against the Oakland A's. This time, Gibson was in bad shape. He had injured both knees in the NL Championship Series and was not in the lineup that day. The A's led 4-3 going into the ninth with their best closer, Dennis Eckersley. With 2 outs, Dodger's Mike Davis got on with a walk to put the tie runner on base.

Gibson came up to the plate after convincing manager Tommy Lasorda he could pinch hit. Everyone in the stadium could see Gibson was in great pain. With his first few cuts he was barely able to slap the ball foul. Every swing looked painful. The hobbling star gallantly hung in there and worked Eckersley to a full count. Eckersley pitched a ball that was drifting towards the outside of the plate. Gibson leaned over using mostly his wrists to swing the bat with just enough power to pop the ball over the fence for the win. Dodgers' stadium erupted and the cheers continued for a long time. Despite his disappointments, Gibson had a big role in two World Series.

Before the New Millennium

The 1990s was a time when people looked back at the past and wondered what the future held. Baseball carried on, but on August 12, 1994, a players' strike began and resulted in the cancellation of the remainder of the season. The postseason was cancelled as well including the World Series. Before 1994, the last year that no World Series took place was 1904.

CURVEBALL QUIZ

He played in 2,632 consecutive games.. Who is Major League Baseball's "IRON MAN"?

ANSWER ON FOLLOWING PAGE

[Curveball Quiz Solution: Cal Ripken Jr.]

The Atlanta Braves were an exciting, talented team in the 1990s. Originating in Boston, the Braves moved to Milwaukee in 1953 and then on to Atlanta in 1966. In 1976, the team was purchased by Ted Turner, owner of TBS, TNT, CNN, Turner Classic Movies, and other media properties. Under Turner, the team became highly competitive and enjoyed a large viewing audience that was supported by Turner's other companies. In the 1990s, the Atlanta Braves would play in five World Series and win one in 1995 against the Cleveland Indians.

In the 1990s, the Braves pitching was brilliant with three future Hall of Famers: Gregg Maddux, Tom Glavine, and John Smoltz. Maddux won four Cy Young Awards, Glavine won two, and Smoltz won one.

In addition to all that pitching talent, was another future hall of famer, third baseman Chipper Jones. Jones was a critical contributor when the Braves won the World Series title in 1995. In 1999, he hit a career-high 45 home runs and he was the NL Most Valuable Player. Jones career would continue with the Braves until 2012. Managing all that talent was Bobby Cox who would join his players in the Hall of Fame as well.

Also in the 1990s, the Toronto Blue Jays won back to back World Series in 1992 and 1993. In the 1992 World Series, Toronto faced the Atlanta Braves. When the Blue Jays won in six games, they became the first team outside the United States to win a World Series. Jays starting pitcher Jack Morris had 21 wins that season. In the 1993 World Series, the Jays beat the Philadelphia Phillies in six games.

The Baltimore Orioles Cal Ripken Jr. ended his record-breaking consecutive games streak on September 20, 1998, with a final tally of 2,632 consecutive games.

Major League Baseball returned to more conventional results towards the end of the decade when the Yankees won the series in 1998 against the San Diego Padres and in 1999 when the Yankees beat the Atlanta Braves.

Conflicts in the Middle East

For most Americans the Middle East is an area that is difficult to understand. Creation of the State of Israel, various wars in the region, and disputes among the countries in the area and their allies have made the region one of the most contentious areas in the world. At the same time, with the growth of the importance of petroleum products and the area's rich resources of oil, most leading nations of the world have a keen interest in the area. Interest or actions from outside the area have increased the exportation of terrorists groups and activities in many places around the world. For the United States, disputes in the Middle East and terrorism aimed at Americans have resulted in various military actions that have escalated into long, drawn-out conflicts in Iraq and Afghanistan.

For Americans, significant military sacrifices have been made in the area. Significant financial sacrifices are made as well. Casualties from the War in Iraq and Afghanistan now number over 59,000.

For Americans, baseball continues through the toughest of times. This is not to show a callous attitude to sacrifice and suffering, but to demonstrate our resolve to maintain the things we value.

CURVEBALL QUIZ

This 6 foot 10 inch pitcher, nicknamed the "Big Unit", threw fastballs that often exceeded 100 miles per hour!

ANSWER ON FOLLOWING PAGE

[Curveball Quiz Solution: Randy Johnson]

21st Century Baseball

Americans woke up one day and the calendar told them that they were living in the 21st century. Disasters that were predicted in the recent and ancient past did not occur. The first day of the 21st century was a lot like the last day of the 20th century. But as time moves on there are many changes taking place.

First Decade

In baseball, the 21st century began with a jump in hitting. A record 5,693 home runs were hit during the 2000 regular season. In the World Series, the Yankees defeated the Mets in five games to win their third consecutive championship. Derek Jeter was the World Series MVP.

Like most activities of 2001, baseball was impacted by the terrorist attacks on America on the morning of Tuesday, September 11, 2001. The attacks pushed back the end of the regular-season from September 30 to October 7.

The Yankees faced the Diamondbacks in the 2001 World Series. Curt Schilling and Randy Johnson of the Diamondbacks were winning pitchers in the first two games in Arizona. No one knew what to expect when the teams returned to New York. In New York, tremendous suffering resulted when the Twin Towers had been targeted about 7 weeks before the series. There were fears a new attack might be perpetrated for the series games in New York. But the city came together with a sense of pride and courage—life would go on after the tragedy and Americans would do what they could to support each other. Incredibly, the Yankees won the next three games in New York by one run in each contest. Those three games infused much needed life and joy into the "Big Apple."

When the series returned to Arizona, the Diamondbacks showed that they were equal to the challenge by evening up the series with a big 15–2 win. In the final game of the series, the Diamondbacks prevailed, 3–2.

The Yankees were in the World Series four different times in the decade. In addition to their 2000 championship, they would also win one in 2009 from the Phillies. The Yankees arch-rival Red Sox won the series in 2004 against the Cardinals and in 2007 against the Colorado Rockies.

Boston Pitcher Curt Schilling was 21–6 at 38 years old in his 19th season in 2004. Schilling suffered a tendon injury to his foot in the Division Series that the Red Sox won against the Anaheim Angels. The American League Championship Series matched the Red Sox against their old nemesis New York Yankees. Behind in the fourth game, the Red Sox tied it in the bottom of the ninth. In the bottom of the 12th, David Ortiz hit a homer to win. In Game 5, Ortiz drove in the winning run in the 14th. In a temporary surgical fix, Schilling's tendon was stitched in place so he could pitch in Game 6. During the game there was some seepage of blood, but Schilling gave the Red Sox seven innings of solid pitching on the way to another win. The Red Sox won the AL Championship Series and then swept the Cardinals in four games. Schilling pitched in two of those games.

In the 2004 World Series, the Cardinals lost to the Red Sox, but they beat the Tigers in 2006. The Phillies beat the Tampa Bay Rays in 2008.

New Teens

At the start of the decade in 2010, the Minnesota Twins opened their new stadium, Target Field. At the end of the decade in 2019, Major League Baseball celebrated its 150th anniversary.

The San Francisco Giants won the 2010 series against the Rangers, the 2012 series against the Tigers, and the 2014 series against the Royals. Their 2010 World Series Championship was their first since moving from New York to San Francisco in 1958! It didn't take them long to win their next one and the next.

Boston fans had much to be thankful for in the decade. The Red Sox won the World Series championship in 2013 against the Cardinals and won again in 2018 against the Dodgers. The Houston Astros beat the Dodgers in 2017, but the Washington Nationals then beat the Astros in 2019. Fans across the country saw highlights of Astros pitcher Justin Verlander throwing his third career no-hitter on September 1, 2019, against the Toronto Blue Jays.

The Washington Nationals have their roots in the Montreal Expos who were established in 1969 and discontinued after the 2004 Season. The franchise moved to Washington, DC, beginning in the 2005 season. In the "teens" (2010-2019), the Nationals had been competitive and won the World Series in 2019. Veteran pitcher Stephen Strasburg was the 2019 World Series MVP. The Nationals were a come-from-behind kind of team that came up through the Wild Card round and won all four World Series games away from home—something that was never done before.

CURVEBALL QUIZ

Among the MLB's best at center field, there is nothing fishy about this Angel's game.

ANSWER ON FOLLOWING PAGE

[Curveball Quiz Solution: Mike Trout]

The Nationals success was all the more remarkable after they had parted company with stellar right fielder Bryce Harper after the 2018 season. Harper moved on to the Phillies where he signed one of those "biggest contracts in the history of the game." Harper had been NL Rookie of the Year in 2012 and MVP in 2015. Pitchers handle Harper with great care; he was walked 130 times in 2018.

The 2020 Season

Baseball has experienced challenges like players' strikes, war, economic depression, earthquakes, and more. But no one would have imagined a season like the 2020 season that worked around the COVID-19 (Coronavirus) Pandemic. Major League Baseball scheduled 60 games for the 2020 regular season. Each Club played 40 games against intra-division opponents and 20 interleague games. The athletes played to empty stadiums, but the games helped take the fan's mind off their troubles via radio, television, and the internet. In 2020, baseball said "life goes on."

Negro Leagues

Players of color participated in early baseball, but only a small number of blacks, Hispanics, and American Indians played. After the Civil War, the country faced the task of bringing the Confederate States back into the Union and resolving many questions relating to the newly emancipated black men and women. This period was called the Reconstruction (1863-1877).

The Reconstruction Amendments are the Thirteenth, Fourteenth, and Fifteenth Amendments to the United States Constitution. The Thirteenth

Amendment (1865) abolished slavery. The Fourteenth Amendment (1868) addressed citizenship rights and equal protection of the laws for all persons. The Fifteenth Amendment (1870) prohibited discrimination in voting rights of citizens on the basis of race, color, or previous condition of servitude.

The effect of these amendments was affected by state laws and court decisions that followed. What resulted was a political and social disaster that led to violence and failed to resolve the racial problems in America. Almost a century later, substantial Civil Rights legislation was passed and the courts addressed weaknesses in the laws that had circumvented the initial intent of the Reconstruction.

Baseball failed as well. The prohibition of players because of race began when in 1884 Chicago player/manager Cap Anson gave a message to his team's owner and General Manager Albert Spalding. The message was that the players of the Chicago "White Stockings" (later, the "Cubs") had decided they would not play in an exhibition game versus the Minor League Toledo Mud Hens if the Mud Hens played Moses Fleetwood "Fleet" Walker their right-fielder, an African-American. According to *A. G. Spalding and the Rise of Baseball*, Albert Spalding eventually obliged, sending a telegram to the Mud Hen's management. Demands like this took their toll. By the 1890's Walker and other black skinned players were gone from the National League.

Negro teams operated in the early days of baseball independent of Major League Baseball. Some of these teams' histories have come to light from work begun in the early 1970s and it continues today. The most famous Negro League and teams began operating in 1920.

The prohibition was tested at times as players from places like Cuba would occasionally have their backers in the states. The prohibition died when Jackie Robinson was recruited to play for the Brooklyn Dodgers in 1947 just after WWII.

The Negro League teams included some established powerhouses like the "Homestead Greys" from Pittsburgh and the Monarchs from Kansas City. They began in 1920 after the end of WWI. Major League players recognized the outstanding play of many African Americans and in the 1930s were inviting them to play in off-season games. These games were part of the unofficial "barn-storming" tours organized by players to make money in the off-season. These teams toured the United States as well as internationally. Some players played in winter leagues in *Cuba*, *Puerto Rico*, *Dominican Republic*, Venezuela, and Mexico in the winter off-season.

Barnstorming and foreign leagues allowed black players to show their talent and engage in some of baseball's earliest global expansion in foreign countries. For example, in 1934 a trip to Japan led by future Hall of Famers including Babe Ruth, Lou Gehrig, and Jimmie Foxx was hugely successful. But a similar team of black players called "The Royal Giants" had already toured Japan in 1927. It featured future Hall of Fame catcher Biz Mackey and pitcher Andy Cooper. Mackey is considered by some as among the greatest defensive catchers ever. He was also a mentor to Brooklyn Dodger African American catcher Roy Campanella when he was with the Baltimore Elite Giants before coming to the Dodgers. The team itself was revered in Japan because they treated the Japanese with great respect teaching them the game. The team won 24 out of 25 exhibition games, with the other being a disputed tie game. As a result, the Japanese players and the fans fell in love with them. Many credit this for sparking the heightened popularity of professional baseball that has continued in Japan, and now South Korea, Taiwan, and Australia. Many players from these leagues have been recruited to play in Major League Baseball, such as Ichiro Suzuki and Yu Darvish.

Just prior to allowing Black players to play in Major League Baseball, a league in Mexico recruited many American players. The league signed many black players and paid good salaries to them because of their talent. In 1938 the renowned Satchel Paige signed to play. In addition, along with Paige, Monte Irvin, Roy Campanella, Josh Gibson, and Cool Papa Bell were among the legendary players to play in the Mexican League. Teams from the league would traditionally travel to Havana to play a fall series against Cuban League teams. Indeed, starting as early as 1906, African American players were signed to play in the Cuban Winter League.

Many great players such as Satchell Paige served as good-will ambassadors for baseball to the world. This is because their grace, ability, and perseverance in the face of discrimination left a global legacy for baseball, a game they loved to play.

Drama of Baseball

Baseball games are dramatic. Everyone can see the hitter is in the *batter's box* and the pitcher on the *pitching mound*. On every pitch, you hear the "whack" of the bat against the ball or "fwomp" of the ball as it hits the catcher's glove. The umpire grunts and calls loudly, "Stee-riiike" when a strike is called.

Each time someone comes to bat, it is a contest between the pitcher and batter. When you play baseball, you know that often you will make an out. If you pitch, you will throw good pitches and bad pitches. In the field, you may make many good catches, but you will miss some, too. Baseball is a game of ups and downs—sometimes you play well—sometimes you don't. We can learn much about life from baseball.

Baseball players can't worry about failing. Every hitter in baseball who fails 70% of the time will still have a .300 batting average, which is considered good. A baseball team that loses a lot of games may still be the first place team. Baseball teaches you that it's ok to fail—everyone does at times. It also teaches you not to worry about failing because you have to move on to the next play. There is no time to think about bad plays in baseball. It's best that way. You keep thinking about what's ahead of you not behind you.

Baseball's Popularity

The president of the United States has often been one of the top fans of the game. Former President Barack Obama threw out the first pitch in a Washington Nationals opening day in 2010. *President George W. Bush* once served as president of the Texas Rangers. His father, *President George H.W. Bush*, was captain of his college squad at Yale University.

The tradition of the "seventh inning stretch" began when *President William Howard Taft* was attending a game in 1910. He was a big man, and he stood to stretch his legs after the top half of the seventh inning of a game. The crowd thought the president was leaving the game, and out of respect they stood up too. They were surprised when the president stuck around and sat down. They sat down too, but the fans decided to continue to get up at the same time to stretch their legs in games that followed. If it was good for the president, it was good for them, too!

Baseball's Measuring Sticks–Statistics

How does baseball measure performance? One of the ways is the use of statistics generated by keeping score of the game as it is being played. The first "Box Score," the chart that tracks player success in an individual game, dates back to baseball's earliest days. The recording of the number of at-bat chances is important. The more chances at-bat, the more valued the player. Likewise, the more hits a player makes when getting the opportunity, the more valuable the player. A player's "batting average" over a season of play is simply determined by dividing the number of hits by the number of at-bats. For example, if in 100 at bats a player has 30 hits, his batting average is .300 (30 divided by 100 = .300).

Then there are other areas of play that complete the measure of performance. This includes measuring the power of a hitter by a formula that includes a batter's singles, doubles, triples, and home runs called the "slugging percentage." For this measure, a single counts as 1 hit, a double counts as 2 hits, a triple counts as 3 hits, and a home run counts as 4 hits. So in our example of 100 at bats, if a player had out of his 30 hits 16 singles, 8 doubles, 2 triples, and 4 home runs, the total of hits would be 16 singles (16 x 1) plus 16 (8 x 2) for doubles, plus 6 (2 x 3) for triples, plus 16 (4 x 4) for home runs. The hits for determining slugging percentage would be 16 +16 +6 + 16 = 54. The result, 54 divided by 100 at bats equals a slugging percentage of .540.

The record for highest slugging percentage ever is .847. It is held by Babe Ruth. Playing in his first year with the Yankees in 1920, in 142 games over the season he had 172 hits, of which 73 were singles, 36 were doubles, 9 were triples, and 54 were home runs. Babe Ruth also holds the career record with a lifetime slugging percentage of .690, a record only approached by Ted Williams' .634 mark, a distant runner-up.

A player is also valued by how many runs he scores. In order to score a lot of runs as compared to other players, the player has to get on base first. So the number of runs scored can be a measure of a player's effectiveness even if it requires another player to drive them home to score. The all-time leader in runs scored is Hall of Famer Ricky Henderson, who played mostly for the Oakland Athletics, among several teams in his long career. He is known for once saying, "If my uniform didn't get dirty I haven't done anything in a baseball game." To measure how well a player hits in scoring opportunities, baseball keeps track how often a hitter drives in a run when another player is in scoring position. This measure is called "runs batted in" or "RBIs" for short.

There are other plays of importance that baseball tracks to measure performance. For example, how often does a player reach base by getting a "walk." Walks, although beneficial, do not count as hits. But they also do not count as 'at-bats' either when it comes to determining the batting average.

How often does a player advance a runner to the next base by intentionally making an out, such as placing a bunt, or by hitting a fly ball to the outfielder that scores a runner? These are called, "sacrifices." But because the hitter in these situations is making something positive happen, but not fully trying to get a hit, in fairness these are not included in the player's at bats when determining his hitting "average."

Another scoring challenge is what to do when a player reaches base on an error. Reaching base on an error is counted as an at-bat, but not as a hit.

Pitching statistics measure the quality of the pitcher. The most important of these is Wins and Losses. A starting pitcher earns a "win" if he pitches at least 5 innings and his team takes a lead for good even if he does not finish the game. If a team is behind in the score when the starting pitcher leaves and his team does not recover the lead or come back to tie the score, the starting pitcher is charged with a loss.

A relief pitcher can pick up the win if the starting pitcher pitches fewer than five innings in what would have been the starter's win, and the official scorer deems that reliever to have been the "most effective" in preserving the win. A pitcher in relief who comes into the game when the score is tied, or the team is behind, but the team ends up winning is awarded the win. When a relief pitcher comes into the game with the lead or the score tied, but the team ends up losing, that pitcher is also the "Losing Pitcher." Each game has only one Winning Pitcher and one Losing Pitcher.

The next statistic in importance is determining "Earned Run Average" (ERA). This is a measure that shows how many runs a pitcher may yield per game over a season. However, to be fair, when a pitcher yields a run that is the fault of a fielder making an error, that run is not counted against the pitcher's earned run average. These are counted as "unearned runs." To determine the ERA, the total number of "earned runs" scored on a pitcher is divided by the innings pitched and then this number is multiplied by 9 (the number of innings in a regular game). For example, if a pitcher has given up 50 earned runs over 100 innings, his average earned run per inning is .50 (50/100). That number is then multiplied by 9 to get the ERA (.50 x 9 equals 4.5).

Scorers also count innings pitched, walks, and strikeouts to round out a rough calculation of overall performance.

Another category modern baseball has developed to measure pitchers who only pitch in relief to seal a victory is called a "Save." The term save referred to when a pitcher entered the game with a lead and finished off a win. Rules now spell out its use. According to Major League Baseball, a relief pitcher recording a save must preserve his team's lead while doing **one** of the following: 1. Enter the game with a lead of no more than three runs and pitch at least one inning. 2. Enter the game with the tying run in the on-deck circle, at the plate or on the bases. 3. Pitch at least three innings. The more "Saves" the more valuable the pitcher.

There are other statistics tracked in the score book, like stolen bases, passed balls by a catcher and wild pitches that advance base runners. By the end of the season, these numbers give fans most of the information to turn actual performance on the field into reasonable ways to compare players over the course of the season. Also, because the basic rules of the game have remained constant for over 120 years since the era of modern Major League Baseball, these statistics help fans measure the value of a player across generations of players.

Superstition in Baseball

"Superstition" has been present since baseball's beginnings. Often it's a questionable action that seems to stir-up curses or bad luck. In other cases, it is used to explain events with reasons created long after the fact that have little basis in truth. The Boston Red Sox experienced a long drought in World Series play after their owner Harry Frazee sold Babe Ruth's services to the New York Yankees. Decades later, Frazee was blamed for the drought in a bit of creative writing, with the reason being identified as "The Curse of the Bambino." Bambino was a nickname for Ruth. At the time of the Ruth sale, many thought Frazee had not done anything wrong.

For modern fans, the "Bambino" curse was recalled again in the media when Boston first baseman Bill Buckner muffed a tricky, spinning ground ball in the 10th inning of Game 6 of the 1986 World Series. The error allowed the New York Mets to stave off elimination. The Mets came back the next game to win the series. But the truth is that Buckner, who had been a great player for the Red Sox, had been ailing with various injuries to his legs making even a routine ground ball difficult. Despite several other chances, the Red Sox were unable to win a World Series until 2003. Why did the drought happen? Who knows, but it was easier and more colorful to explain it with the "Curse of the Bambino" than finding the truth buried in decades of games, long lines of managers and players, and statistics.

The Chicago Cubs went without winning a World Series for over 100 years and didn't win a pennant from 1946 until 2016. The reasons behind the 100+ year drought on the series is a little murky, but the lack of a pennant win and World Series Championship after 1945 was blamed on the "Billy-Goat Curse." Local restauranteur William Sianis of the Billy Goat Tavern brought his goat to Wrigley Field to roam the outfield for good luck before the World Series against the Detroit Tigers in 1945. The Cubs sent the goat home and born was the "Billy-Goat Curse:" the Cubs would not win a

World Series until the goat was allowed back in. "Lovable Losers" became the nickname for the team. Despite reports of a goat coming back to graze occasionally in Wrigley Field, it took until 2016 to "break" the curse. Cubs Manager at the time, Joe Maddon, expressed absolute disdain for the curse and said his players would excel regardless. The Cubs made good on the promise and beat the Cleveland Indians in seven games in the 2016 World Series.

Many "rituals" are employed by ballplayers to give themselves good luck or to avoid bad luck. Sometimes a batter hits the ball hard, but right at a fielder for an out. Some might say, "He was 'snake bit." When it happens to others, the whole team might be "snake bit." But teammates must believe that better innings lie ahead if they keep hitting the ball on the nose and hard! Soon the hits will start coming!

In the on-deck circle, Ty Cobb always swung three bats. Not a weighted bat, or just two bats. To warm-up, Native American pitcher Chief Bender of the Philadelphia Athletics never threw to any catcher other than Ira Thomas.

In a book called *Batting* by F. C. Lane, Hall of Fame player Eddie Collins put it this way:

"The ball player has seen too many games decided by some freak play not to have a profound respect for the element of luck in the game. Most players will admit to you that you must get the breaks to win. Now in plain English the 'breaks' constitute that unknown element in every game which a player recognizes clearly enough but cannot guard against...superstition. For after all, superstition is only an attempt to provide for something that cannot be foreseen. Ballplayers usually respect each other's superstitions, even when they appear most foolish."

The great Ty Cobb once recalled a season in Detroit when a stray dog wandered into the clubhouse and became the Tigers omen of good fortune.

"He was a friendly sort of mutt, and I couldn't seem to shake him. He came willingly enough, wagging his tail and making friends with all the ball players. We left him in the clubhouse, went out and won the game. In fact, we had great luck that series. So we decided to show some appreciation of the mutt. We christened him 'Victory.' Then we went to Washington, and 'Victory' was so much a part of our schedule that we took him out on the bench. The team lost the series opening game however, and he seemed to be of more use to us in the clubhouse instead of the bench. The next day we left him in the clubhouse, and sure enough we won. He was in the clubhouse when we played the Athletics and we took the series handily. The same continued in the next series at home in Detroit. But the next road trip, the trainer who became his keeper, forgot to bring him. I knew nothing about it. I was ready to fire him. The boys were pretty upset about it when we lost. So you see from all of this that ball players are really not superstitious. They simply have curious ideas about some things."

Superstition undoubtedly affects the work of many hitters. Cleveland Indian Hall of Famer Tris Speaker said before every at bat he drew a line with his bat at the top of the batter's box. He said it started when he was in the Minor Leagues. In the Minors, often for the batter's box, the lines were not drawn. So he would make them in the dirt. He stayed with it in the Major League even though the lines were there. The ritual calmed him. Then he was ready to hit. He controlled his timing, not the pitcher. Cubs Hall of Famer Billy Williams before every at bat would spit and do a practice swing to his spittle. It did the same for him.

Other taboos abound. When losing late in a game, it is considered bad luck to start putting all the equipment away until the game is over. Who knows? If a pitcher is throwing a no-hitter or perfect game, savvy players and coaches do not mention it on the bench. Announcers in the broadcast booth are often careful not to jinx a performance with too much direct conversation about a potential no-hitter or perfect game.

When it comes to superstition, players decide how much or how little provide a routine that provides confidence.

Make a New Plan

In the early 1900s, Joe McCarthy was determined to become a Major League Baseball player. At that time, thousands of athletes saw their parents work long hours in factories, industrial plants, mills, and mines. Baseball was an opportunity for a different life. A baseball player was out in the fresh air working to improve baseball skills and knowledge while playing a game. A baseball player was using his abilities to make a living doing something he loved to do.

McCarthy did not make it in the Majors, but he sure tried. He played in the Minor Leagues for over 15 years traveling around on hot buses, staying in cheap hotels, and earning a small salary. It must have been humbling, some might have thought of him a *bush leaguer*. Yet, he did enjoy what he was doing. More importantly, he learned from many different coaches and players.

McCarthy played for several different Minor League teams. They had interesting names: the Wilmington Colts, the Franklin Millionaires, the Toledo Mud Hens, the Coal-Barons of Wilkes-Barre, the Buffalo Bisons, and the Louisville Colonels. Although McCarthy finally had to admit that he was not quite good enough to play in the Major League, he made a new plan and became a terrific Major League manager.

McCarthy managed four of the most famous baseball players of all time: Babe Ruth, Lou Gehrig, Joe DiMaggio, and Ted Williams. He managed the Chicago Cubs, taking them from last place to the National League Pennant. He managed the New York Yankees for 15 years and won seven World Series. The last team he managed was the Boston Red Sox.

About 100 years ago, McCarthy wrote down what he thought were the important principles to follow when playing baseball. He called these the *10 Commandments of Baseball*. You may never have heard of McCarthy, but chances are if you had a good coach, your coach taught you some of his baseball principles or what we call Baseball's Winning Ways in this book.

Some people might think that reading about players from the past is not important today, but they are wrong. In baseball, the past is studied and respected. Ted Williams was a great student of hitting and his book, *The Science of Hitting*, is still read today 50 years after its original publication. Many players are trained on techniques that Williams developed.

CURVEBALL QUIZ

Who is the patient and popular manager named most valuable manager in both the NL and AL?

ANSWER ON FOLLOWING PAGE

[Curveball Quiz Solution: Joe Maddon.]

Babe Ruth helped save professional baseball when it looked like it might not survive. New biographies of Ruth appear even today. Many of today's great players are inspired by Jackie Robinson, Henry Aaron, Willie Mays, and Roberto Clemente. Baseball today would not be the same game without these and other great men.

Winning Ways

The winning ways of baseball discussed here are taken from Joe McCarthy's *10 Commandments of Baseball.* These are perhaps the most fundamental principles or qualities that have been taught by good coaches for many decades.

Nobody ever became a ballplayer by walking after a ball.

Hustle. Ballplayers should approach each small task with energy and strength. Possessing a winning attitude instills a little fun into all our efforts. We attract other winning people and surround ourselves with teammates and others who will help our cause.

You will never become a .300 hitter unless you take the bat off your shoulder.

Act. No doubt about it, the folks at Nike really said a lot when they said, "Just do it." Just do it without fear of failure, fear of embarrassment, and without thinking we cannot do it. Act with courage and not doubt. Encourage others to do the same, just imagine how much we can accomplish. Inspire others to succeed.

An outfielder who throws back of a runner is locking the barn after the horse is stolen.

Make the right play is what this principle means. There are times for taking risks; there are times to cut our losses. Some situations are easier to manage than others, but we need to play to our strengths and manage our game. Certainly, there are times for us to stretch out and grow. Other times we need to take our lumps.

Keep your head up and you may not have to keep it down.

Stay positive. Good things come to those who are alert and those who look ahead and anticipate. We learn by paying attention to what is going on around us and to what other people are saying. If we do not listen to others, they will not listen to us. If we do not keep our head in the game, we will not be playing the game. The game will be playing us.

When you start to slide, S–L–I–D–E. He who changes his mind may have to change a good leg for a bad one.

Be Decisive. In baseball, hesitating after you have seemingly made a decision often has immediate payback. In life, it can be more subtle. Rules can be made in haste and then not enforced. Promises can be made and not kept. Decisions can be made and remade and remade again. We need to make our decisions and articulate them to others clearly. All indecisive and inconsistent behaviors hurt us and those around us.

Do not alibi on bad hops. Anybody can field the good ones.

No Excuses–learn the difficult. Honesty and humility, followed by determination to improve, are a great recipe for success. We need to take responsibility to complete our tasks and reach our goals. Not accepting responsibility for one's actions and blaming others is a great recipe for failure.

Always run them out. You can never tell.

Never Give In. A determined effort is a 100% effort, not a 90% effort or an 80% effort. Baseball is a game of inches and hundredths of seconds. Life is no different. Practice the fundamentals, keep training for the big game, and develop your talents and those of others around you.

Do not quit.

Don't give up. As *Yogi Berra* said, "it ain't over 'til it's over." In baseball, many games are won after thousands of spectators have left because a game "looked like it was all over," but it was not. How much would life be different if we just did not quit? We need to keep striving to earn success.

Do not find too much fault with the umpires. You cannot expect them to be as perfect as you are.

Honor Authority. Making the call or judgement is what coaches, umpires and others in authority do in sports. People who live long and successful lives, say that judging others comes back to haunt those who are not called on to judge. Respect the authorities and let them do their job.

A pitcher who hasn't control, hasn't anything.

Practice Self-control. Life is challenging. We need to be at our best. We need to treat ourselves and others with respect and avoid self-destructive habits. Self-control brings victories.

Benjamin Franklin

Ben Franklin's Chart on Virtues

About the time our country was getting started, Ben Franklin, one of our country's founding fathers and "thought leaders," wrote about creating virtuous habits. This information was part of the *Autobiography of Ben Franklin*, one of the greatest books ever written.

Franklin was not only a great thinker, he was accomplished in many pursuits. Franklin knew that he needed to work on forming good habits if he was going to improve and accomplish goals. As a means of self-help, Franklin created sheets that he used to record his work on virtues. Franklin created a list of virtues that he identified through his reading and research: temperance, silence, order, resolution, frugality, industry, sincerity, justice, moderation, cleanliness, tranquility, chastity, and humility.

Franklin wanted to focus on one virtue for at least a week. He wanted to create a habit practicing the virtue. He created a weekly chart with the name of one virtue and its definition at the top. Below the virtue, written or printed in a row, he created a square or cell for each day of the week. Then he included a column running down the left side of the chart with the first letter of all the virtues. The chart was filled out with blank boxes or cells. Each evening, he examined his conscience and he checked the boxes adjacent to the virtues where his performance was weak. He examined each virtue every day, but his focus was doing well on the "virtue of the week."

CURVEBALL QUIZ
Who are the three MLB baseball brothers that are all catchers and all have World Series rings?
ANSWER ON FOLLOWING PAGE

[Curveball Quiz Solution: Molina brothers: Yadier, Bengie and José.]

Baseball's Winning Ways Charts

Focus on one virtue each week and every night take some time to evaluate how you did. If you need to improve, place a check mark in the box under the day of the week you are "grading" in the row for that virtue. For days when you did well, put a star. For the first week, you are focusing on "Hustle," but go ahead and mark how you did for the other virtues as well.

Week One

For the first week, each night you might ask yourself: Did I approach each task with energy and strength?

Hustle Approach tasks with energy.							
	S	M	T	W	T	F	S
H							
A							
R							
P							
D							
E							
I							
U							
H							
S							

H-Hustle, A-Act, R-Make the Right Play, P-Stay Positive, D-Be Decisive, E-Make No Excuse, I-Never Give In (100% effort, always), U-Never Give Up, H-Honor Authority, S-Practice Self Control.

Week Two

For the second week, each night you might ask yourself: Did I take action when it was needed?

Act Don't let fear of failure hold you back.							
	S	M	T	W	T	F	S
A							
R							
P							
D							
E							
I							
U							
H							
S							
H							

A-Act, R-Make the Right Play, P-Stay Positive, D-Be Decisive, E-Make No Excuse, I-Never Give In (100% effort, always), U-Never Give Up, H-Honor Authority, S-Practice Self Control, H-Hustle.

Week Three

For the third week, each night you might ask yourself: Did I make the right play or did I act recklessly?

Make the Right Play Do what the situation calls for you to do.							
	S	M	T	W	T	F	S
R							
P							
D							
E							
I							
U							
H							
S							
H							
A							

R-Make the Right Play, P-Stay Positive, D-Be Decisive, E-Make No Excuse, I-Never Give In (100% effort, always), U-Never Give Up, H-Honor Authority, S-Practice Self Control, H-Hustle, A-Act.

Week Four

For the fourth week, each night you might ask yourself: Did I remain positive?

Be Positive Be Positive, Stay Alert.							
	S	M	T	W	T	F	S
P							
D							
E							
I							
U							
H							
S							
H							
A							
R							

P-Stay Positive, D-Be Decisive, E-Make No Excuse, I-Never Give In (100% effort, always), U-Never Give Up, H-Honor Authority, S-Practice Self Control, H-Hustle, A-Act, R-Make the Right Play.

Week Five

For the fifth week, each night you might ask yourself: Was I decisive or was I timid in my actions?

Decisive Make your decision and follow it through.							
	S	M	T	W	T	F	S
D							
E							
I							
U							
H							
S							
H							
A							
R							
P							

D-Be Decisive, E-Make No Excuse, I-Never Give In (100% effort, always), U-Never Give Up, H-Honor Authority, S-Practice Self Control, H-Hustle, A-Act, R-Make the Right Play, P-Stay Positive.

Week Six

For the sixth week, each night you might ask yourself: What excuses did I make today?

No Excuses Make no excuses, do the difficult.							
	S	M	T	W	T	F	S
E							
I							
U							
H							
S							
H							
A							
R							
P							
D							

E-Make No Excuse, I-Never Give In (100% effort, always), U-Never Give Up, H-Honor Authority, S-Practice Self Control, H-Hustle, A-Act, R-Make the Right Play, P-Stay Positive, D-Be Decisive.

Week Seven

For the seventh week, each night you might ask yourself: Did I approach each task with 100% commitment and effort?

Don't Give In Approach tasks with optimum effort.							
	S	M	T	W	T	F	S
I							
U							
H							
S							
H							
A							
R							
P							
D							
E							

I-Never Give In (100% effort, always), U-Never Give Up, H-Honor Authority, S-Practice Self Control, H-Hustle, A-Act, R-Make the Right Play, P-Stay Positive, D-Be Decisive, E-Make No Excuse.

Week Eight

For the eighth week, each night you might ask yourself: What did I give up on today?

Don't Give Up Never quit.							
	S	M	T	W	T	F	S
U							
H							
S							
H							
A							
R							
P							
D							
E							
I							

U-Never Give Up, H-Honor Authority, S-Practice Self Control, H-Hustle, A-Act, R-Make the Right Play, P-Stay Positive, D-Be Decisive, E-Make No Excuse, I-Never Give In (100% effort, always).

Week Nine

For the ninth week, each night you might ask yourself: Did I let those in authority do their job?

Honor Authority Let those in authority do their job without criticism.							
	S	M	T	W	T	F	S
H							
S							
H							
A							
R							
P							
D							
E							
I							
U							

H-Honor Authority, S-Practice Self Control, H-Hustle, A-Act, R-Make the Right Play, P-Stay Positive, D-Be Decisive, E-Make No Excuse, I-Never Give In (100% effort, always), U-Never Give Up.

Week Ten

For the tenth week, each night you might ask yourself: Did I practice self-control?

Practice Self Control Approach tasks with discipline.							
	S	M	T	W	T	F	S
S							
H							
A							
R							
P							
D							
E							
I							
U							
H							

S-Practice Self Control, H-Hustle, A-Act, R-Make the Right Play, P-Stay Positive, D-Be Decisive, E-Make No Excuse, I-Never Give In (100% effort, always), U-Never Give Up, H-Honor Authority.

CURVEBALL QUIZ

One of the best outfielders in baseball, this talented player is also a professional bowler!

ANSWER ON FOLLOWING PAGE

[Curveball Quiz Solution: Mookie Betts]

Making the Cut

Playing sports for a living is something that millions of young people would like to achieve. But only a small number *make the cut*. And yet, many people do make their living in sports and fitness. Today, we know how important it is for people to stay fit and take good care of themselves. Regardless of what you do for a living, if you are fit, you will do it better.

In every community there are physical education instructors at schools, coaches and assistants; trainers, gym managers and staff; referees; managers of sports organizations and associations; and many others involved in sports. There are also sports therapists, doctors who specialize in treating sports injuries; sports reporters; sports announcers; sports lawyers; sports marketing professionals; and sports information directors.

An athlete may want to succeed in professional sports as a player, but there are plenty of opportunities in sports. Former athletes and sports enthusiasts can also make their living by working outside of sports, but find sports opportunities in volunteer work.

Education

If you decide to seek sports as a living, you will need education. Much has happened in sports education in the past several decades. The education and training you seek will say something about the knowledge, skills, and abilities you have to serve others. Sports careers can require a high school diploma all the way up to a successful *medical internship*.

CURVEBALL QUIZ

Which Brewer hit for the cycle twice in 2018?

ANSWER ON FOLLOWING PAGE

[Curveball Quiz Solution: Christian Yelich]

Playing Fair

Winning in baseball sometimes takes advantage of circumstances. An outfielder might shift towards the line for a pull hitter. A runner on first might take a bigger leadoff if the pitcher's pickoff move is below average. But trying to take advantage of every situation can lead to "bending" the rules. However, "lies don't last." Playing fair is the only "winning way."

Benjamin Franklin humorously wrote about the difficulty of keeping a secret in *Poor Richard's Almanac.* "Three may keep a secret, if two of them are dead." Franklin also wrote in the same publication: "A lie stands on one leg, truth on two."

In baseball the catcher signals to a pitcher suggesting a certain type of pitch. Sometimes an instruction might be sent using a signal from the bench. Signals are also used in other circumstances such as when a coach directs a base runner to hold up on base or keep running after another batter has hit the ball.

Teams have made an effort over the years to attempt to read the signals given to the pitcher and let the hitter know what type of pitch he might expect. This is called "stealing the signs" and has been tolerated to a point. Usually, when such sign stealing has taken place in past, the team on the field realizes it and changes the signs to counter the "theft."

One problem in sports today is that modern technology can lend a hand to cheating that is not only hard to detect, but that produces disastrous results. Just as football teams have used certain technologies to spy on other teams in practice, baseball signals can be read with technological devices and with more accuracy. One result has been great damage to good pitching performance. When cheating takes place the results are undeserved wins and losses that are near impossible to correct. Sign stealing is something Major League Baseball is focused on now because it threatens fair play.

Great pitchers like Warren Spahn have maintained that throwing off a batter's timing is a secret to successful pitching. When a batter is notified in advance of the type of pitch he is about to see, the pitcher loses a tremendous advantage.

Another way of cheating is the use of steroids to artificially improve muscle and strength. Often the perpetrator is caught when a random test is performed or a person identified as delivering the drug is caught. The supplier or source often implicates a group of athletes that have participated. At first, denials are made, but at some point, typically an admission is made and punishment is doled out. Fair play wins out.

Unfortunately for everyone, when performance enhancing drugs are used, the game and the athlete is soiled. No matter how well the athlete plays afterward; how good a guy he is in the field as well as at the plate hitting; how well liked he is in the clubhouse as a teammate; he carries with him a stigma to his reputation. For baseball itself, team performance, records, and achievements come under suspicion. In a game that prides itself with careful tracking of records and performance, certain records are now and forever under suspicion. For the compromised players, they may never receive awards and honors that typically accompany their achievements such as being voted into the National Baseball Hall of Fame. For players opposing the steroid-using athlete, their personal records and success have been affected.

Another serious threat to all sports is illegal betting. Baseball barely survived a situation in 1919 when seven key players, including All-Star Shoeless Joe Jackson, took money from gamblers to intentionally lose the World Series against the Cincinnati Reds. These players were banned from baseball for life. An eighth player, star shortstop Buck Weaver, who did not take any of the pay-off money, was still banned for life because he knew about the scam, but said nothing about it to any authority to stop it. Over the years, since the 1919 White Sox scandal, some players and coaches have been implicated in betting. In some cases, an admission of guilt comes with a statement that the bets made never affected outcomes or performance. But when gambling rules are broken, the ultimate effect is never completely understood.

CURVEBALL QUIZ
CLANG!
Who hit a 500ft. blast that clanked off the replica Liberty Bell in Philly's Vet Stadium in 1972?
ANSWER ON THE FOLLOWING PAGE

[Curveball Quiz Solution: Greg Luzinski]

Glossary

$100,000 Infield

The $100,000 infield played for Connie Mack's Philadelphia Athletics in the Dead ball era, at a time when the team was winning pennants. A reporter's question to Connie Mack along the lines, "Would you accept $100,000 to trade your tremendous infield?" Connie replied, "No." So they became the "$100,000 infield." The group consisted of Stuffy McInnis, Eddie Collins, Jack Barry, and Frank Baker. In 1910, 1911, and 1913 they won the World Series. The foursome was broken up in 1915.

10 Commandments of Baseball

Joe McCarthy wrote up his baseball principles in 1922 while he was coaching in the Minor Leagues.

The 10 Commandments of Baseball

1. Nobody ever became a ballplayer by walking after a ball.
2. You will never become a .300 hitter unless you take the bat off your shoulder.
3. An outfielder who throws back of a runner is locking the barn after the horse is stolen.
4. Keep your head up and you may not have to keep it down.
5. When you start to slide, S–L–I–D–E. He who changes his mind may have to change a good leg for a bad one.

6. Do not alibi on bad hops. Anybody can field the good ones.
7. Always run them out. You can never tell.
8. Do not quit.
9. Do not find too much fault with the umpires. You cannot expect them to be as perfect as you are.
10. A pitcher who hasn't control, hasn't anything.

Accolades

An accolade was the essential act in the ceremonies conferring knighthood. Accolade is used generally to mean praise or award.

Adversity

Adversity is a series of difficulties or misfortunes that can keep you from reaching your goals or living in a positive way.

A. G. Spalding and the Rise of Baseball

A. G. Spalding and the Rise of Baseball by Peter Levine is a book about one of baseball's early innovators who also produced a staggering amount of baseball information through his books and sold sports equipment through his company. *A. G. Spalding and the Rise of Baseball* is published by Oxford University Press: New York, New York, 1985, 184 pages.

Alibi

When used as a verb, Alibi is to furnish an excuse to avoid blame. When used as a noun, it refers to that thing that presents the excuse. Some players will excuse themselves from catching the bad hops, others will practice until they have the skills to catch them.

All-Star Game

All-Star Game is an annual baseball game between selected professional players from the National League and the American League.

ALS

ALS is amyotrophic lateral sclerosis, a disease that affects nerve cells in the brain and the spinal cord. Once called Lou Gehrig Disease after the Hall of Fame player who contracted it. Starting in 2014, the ALS Association topped $115 million in donations from people participating in the "Ice Bucket Challenge."

Autobiography of Ben Franklin

Franklin began writing his Autobiography in 1771 and worked on it sporadically until shortly before his death in 1790. It was published in various languages and versions beginning in 1791, but the complete Autobiography of Benjamin Franklin, including Franklin's final revisions, did not appear until 1868. The work comprises four sections, reflecting the four different periods during which he wrote it, spanning his life as a youth to his time in the Pennsylvania Assembly in the late 1750s. Franklin never completed what he considered his memoir, but it is, nevertheless, crowded with events, inventions, and his tireless efforts to study morality, philosophy, politics, science, and literature.

Batter's Box

Batter's Box is a designated area that is chalked out where the batter positions himself during his at-bat.

Batting titles

The batting title is awarded to the batter with the leading batting average in each league after the season ends. The National League batting title is known as the "Tony Gwynn Award" and the American League batting title is the "Rod Carew Award" named after Hall of Famers who had won multiple batting titles in their playing career.

Book of Baseball (The)

There are many historic books on baseball, *The Book of Baseball* by William Patten and J. Walker McSpadden is one of the more interesting. This 1911 classic baseball text has recently published in a commemorative 100th Anniversary edition by Dover Publications. *The Book of Baseball* is a guide to professional baseball as it was played a century ago exploring baseball's roots in the 1830s, the origins of the National and American leagues, the art of pitching, star plays and players, umpiring, the Minor Leagues, and many other aspects of our national pastime.

Boston Common

Dating from 1634, Boston Common is the oldest park in the United States. The 50 acre park in downtown Boston has been a gathering place for play and public discourse. Concerts, baseball games, protests, hangings, burials, and historical events have taken place at the Common.

Bush Leaguer

Bush leaguer is a slang term that refers to a baseball player who is not good enough to play in the Major League.

Called his shot

Called his shot refers to the time when Babe Ruth was up to the plate against the Chicago Cubs in Game 3 of the 1932 World Series. Many insist that Ruth pointed to the center-field bleachers as if to suggest he was about to hit the ball in that direction. On the next pitch, Ruth hit a home run to centerfield.

Calling the game

Both the pitcher and catcher study the habits of hitters on other teams. The pitcher is likely focused on his execution and performance. It's thought that the catcher can take some of the pressure off the pitcher by giving signs that suggest what pitch might be thrown. This is referred to as "calling the game."

Caricatures

Caricatures are illustrations or descriptions of a person or people in which certain characteristics are exaggerated in order to create a comic effect.

Central Intelligence Agency

The Central Intelligence Agency of the United States Government monitors foreign intelligence to further national security objectives. Created under the National Security Act of 1947 and signed by President Truman on July 26, 1947, the CIA evolved from various renditions of an intelligence agency prior to its formal establishment. The Agency serves the President by reporting as a civilian foreign intelligence service of the federal government officially tasked with gathering, processing, and analyzing national security information from around the world. It works primarily through the use of human intelligence. Unlike the FBI, it has no power to prosecute.

Chronology

Chronology is the historical ordering of things. Ordering events by when they happened often helps us understand them better and see relationships such as possible causes and effects.

Commendable

Commendable is something that is worthy of praise.

Constitution

The system or body of fundamental rules that govern a State, nation, social, or professional organization.

Contenders

Contenders are people or a team that has seriously entered into a competition with others. A contender is one who has a chance to win, not merely someone who is competing for fun who has no chance. Example: Thousands of people were at the starting line before the Marathon race. Individuals who were identified as contenders based on past race results, were in a separate area and would be starting 10 minutes ahead of the pack.

Cuba

Cuba is a country comprised mostly of the island of Cuba that is located in the northern Caribbean where the Caribbean Sea, Gulf of Mexico and Atlantic Ocean meet. It is east of Mexico, south of Florida and west of Hispaniola where Haiti and the Dominican Republic are found.

Dominican Republic

The Dominican Republic lies on the island of Hispaniola along with Haiti in the Caribbean archipelago known as the Greater Antilles. It is the most populous island in the West Indies. The Dominican Republic is roughly 800 miles from Florida, it is east of Cuba and west of Puerto Rico in the Caribbean Sea.

"Ed Sullivan Show"

The Ed Sullivan Show was a popular TV variety show that was hosted by newspaper entertainment columnist, Ed Sullivan. It ran from 1948 to 1971. Watching the live show was a family ritual each Sunday evening. Guests came from all categories of entertainment and many of the most popular entertainers would perform live on the show.

Elizabethan Era

The Elizabethan Era is the period of the reign of Queen Elizabeth I (1558–1603). Considered a golden age in English history and English literature, it was the time of William Shakespeare and an age of English expansion and exploration.

Farm System

The "farm system" is the working and financial relationship between Minor League baseball teams and Major League clubs. Minor League teams often have an affiliation with a Major League team and they feed players to the team as the players mature. At the same time, Major League teams will often send players "down" to the Minors for extra work and rehab after injuries.

Flying Dutchman

In legend and literature, the Flying Dutchman is a phantom (ghost) ship that can never make port and is doomed to sail the oceans forever. The myth has been used in the arts. The Flying Dutchman was also the nickname given to Honus Wagner. The nickname is an allusion to this myth and an opera composed by the German composer Richard Wagner. Honus Wagner was fast and like the Composer Wagner of German heritage so it fit.

Followed suit

Followed suit is an idiom, an expression that means more than the dictionary definition of its words. Followed suit means doing what someone else has just done.

Foul Strike Rule

In the early days of baseball when a batter hit a foul ball it was not called a strike. The Foul Strike Rule made foul balls strikes unless the batter already had two strikes. The rule was adopted early in the 20th century.

Gold Glove

The Rawlings Gold Glove Award or Gold Glove is an award given annually to the Major League Baseball players judged to have exhibited superior fielding at each position in the National League and the American League. The award is determined by a vote of managers and coaches as well as statistical measures provided by the Society for American Baseball Research (SABR). An annual Platinum Glove Award selected by fans is given to the best defensive player among Gold Glove winners in each league.

"Hitless Wonders"

"Hitless Wonders" is the nickname for the White Sox of 1906. The 1906 World Series matched the Chicago Cubs, who had the most regular-season wins, with the "Hitless Wonders" White Sox, who had the worst team batting average. The Sox beat the Cubs in six games for one of the greatest upsets in series history.

"Hitting the curveball"

The curveball is traditionally one of the most challenging pitches to hit in professional baseball because it moves in unexpected ways. It can be a trial for a player moving up from a lower level of play to make the proper adjustments necessary to hit the pitch at a higher level of play.

"Hitting the curveball" is also an "idiom," an expression that means more than the dictionary definition of its words. Someone who is "hitting the curveball" is succeeding at something that is difficult. Someone who can "hit the curveball" separates himself or herself from others.

Foreign-speaking persons have difficulty with idioms. Normally, a foreign-speaking person must learn the meaning of idioms from experience.

Home Run Derby

Home Run Derby is an annual home run hitting competition in Major League Baseball regularly held the day before the All-Star Game. But kids have been playing their own versions of Home Run Derby for many decades. One common version calls on players to set boundaries in advance from where the ball is batted to the "fence," the "wall," or a line. The batting player throws the ball up himself and hits it intending to send the ball over the point where it yields a home run. Players take turns batting and fielding. Any hit that does not go past the home run mark is an out. A ball that exceeds it is a home run. Many variations exist on the rules of this game, but as few as 2 players can play, making it a popular game when a larger number of kids are not available.

"Hot corner"

The third base position in baseball is referred to as the "hot corner" because for right-handed hitters the distance down the line to third base is a mere 90 feet; balls hit in that direction often come at the third baseman at great speed. The third baseman must possess a strong arm, the ability to move quickly from side to side, and excellent footwork.

Hyperbole

Hyperbole is extravagant exaggeration—not just exaggerating a little bit but exaggerating so much so that people immediately know you are stretching the truth. This is done in sports reporting to entertain.

Incarcerated

People who are put in prison are incarcerated. During wars special prisons are often used because large numbers of soldiers are "taken prisoner." Conditions at some Civil War prisons were so horrible that large numbers of prisoners died from disease, starvation, and exposure.

Instability

Instability is the quality of being unstable or unreliable. People who are unstable, cannot be trusted.

"Iron Horse"

"Iron Horse" was a term used for a steam locomotive that called to mind the fact that these machines were replacing the power of horses to move people and goods. "Iron Horse" became the nickname for Lou Gehrig after he impressed people with his durability and power while playing baseball. His mark for most consecutive games played of 2,130 was a record that held for 56 years.

Legendary

Legendary is famous, renowned, acclaimed, or well known. An event or a person that grows in importance, sometimes becomes legendary. Both real and fictitious events and characters can also become legendary.

Lithography

Lithography is a printing process that uses a flat printing surface (originally a limestone plate) with a hand drawn image on it in which the image to be printed is ink receptive and the blank area is ink repellent.

Luminaries

Luminaries are famous people who have done great things. Luminaries are people of prominence or achievement.

Major League Baseball

Major League Baseball is an organization of the highest level of professional baseball teams in North America (Canada and the United States). Major League Baseball oversees Minor League teams that are affiliated with Major League Teams. Currently there are 15 American League Teams and 15 National League Teams in Major League Baseball. For many years, the American League and National League were separate organizations, but they consolidated into a single entity in 2000.

"Make the Cut"

In many competitive situations whether people are auditioning for movie roles, membership on a team, or attempting to gain a spot in some club or organization, the candidates are eliminated or cut from the selection process until only those chosen remain. When someone is not eliminated, they are said to "make the cut."

Matthias Boutlier

Matthias Boutlier was a Xaverian Religious Brother and the disciplinarian at St. Mary's Industrial School for Boys in Baltimore when Babe Ruth was enrolled. Brother Matthias cared for Babe Ruth and worked hard to see that he was educated and trained. He showed compassion for Ruth who never forgot him.

Medical Internship

Medical Internship is a position or period of supervised medical practice and training for a recently graduated physician that leads to a full license to practice medicine.

Millennium

Millennium is an even 1,000 years or 10 centuries. The new millennium began in the year 2000 and will go on until 2999.

Minor League

Minor League teams belong to an association of teams below the Major League level in which players work to improve their performance so they are ready for the Major League. Minor League teams are often affiliated with a Major League club. They usually play in places of smaller populations than Major League cities. They enjoy a loyal following and offer many of the same types of entertainment as Major League teams. Minor League teams have been in existence for over 100 years.

"Mr. Cub"

"Mr. Cub" was the nickname given Ernie Banks who was an enthusiastic Hall of Fame player and who spent his entire career with the Chicago Cubs team. Many fans, players, and the media thought that Banks was an excellent representative of the team who practiced positive thinking regardless of the Cubs position.

Mutation in Evolution

According to the U.S. Department of Health and Human Services, evolution is the process by which populations of organisms change over generations. Genetic variations underlie these changes. Genetic variations can arise from gene mutations or from genetic recombination (a normal process in which genetic material is rearranged as a cell is getting ready to divide).

Newbery Medal

The Newbery Medal was named for eighteenth-century British bookseller and publisher John Newbery. His Newbery's Publishing Company was among the first to publish children's books like the *Little Pretty Pocket Book*. The Newbery Medal is awarded annually by the Association for Library Service to Children, a division of the American Library Association. This highly coveted award goes to the author of the most distinguished contribution to American literature for children.

Nineteenth Amendment

The Nineteenth Amendment to the U. S. Constitution, ratified in Washington, D.C. on August 19, 1920, provides that all female citizens are entitled to vote.

Perfect Game

In baseball, a perfect game is recorded when a pitcher and his team does not allow any opposing player to reach base by any means.

Pitching Mound

Pitching Mound is a small raised area near the center of the infield from which the pitcher throws the ball. In professional baseball, the distance from the mound to home plate is 60' 6."

Play Ball

"Play ball" is called out by the umpire at the start of a game or after some time out or intermission. In a time out, a player might walk off a base or a batter might leave the batter's box, but once the ump utters the words "play ball," the game is live. "Play ball" is also an idiom meaning "let's get started." In business, one side of a potential contract might be ready to "play ball," meaning they are ready to negotiate.

Polygon

A polygon is a closed figure made up of straight lines joined end to end. A regular polygon is one that is equiangular (all angles are equal) and equilateral (all sides are the same length). An irregular polygon is a polygon that is not regular.

President Barack Obama

The 44th president of the United States, Barack Obama was the first African American to hold the office. The two-term president began his first term in 2009 and his second in 2013. Obama is a graduate of Columbia University and Harvard Law School. Obama worked as a community organizer, practiced law, and taught at the University of Chicago Law School. He served in the U.S. Senate and the Illinois House of Representatives before his election as president.

President Dwight D. Eisenhower

The 34th president of the United States Dwight D. Eisenhower had an extensive military background. During World War II, Eisenhower rose to Supreme Commander of the Allied troops in Europe, planning and conducting the D-Day landings in France. He managed to sustain order and keep a diverse group of generals working together at the most critical point in the war. After the war, he ran for President in 1952 using the slogan, "I like Ike." He served two terms. As president, Eisenhower was credited with easing the tensions of the Cold War. In his youth, Eisenhower was an excellent athlete who played football while attending the United States Military Academy at West Point.

President Franklin Delano Roosevelt

The 32nd President of the United States, Franklin Delano Roosevelt (FDR), was elected to his first of four terms in 1932. He died at the closing moments of World War II in 1945. Roosevelt won election in the early stages of the Great Depression. He implemented policies and programs that were known as the New Deal to improve the economy and reduce the suffering of millions of Americans. Before becoming president, FDR was stricken with polio. He lost the ability to use his legs, but he did not want Americans to focus on his disability so he avoided publicity on it.

He married a distant cousin, Eleanor Roosevelt, who became one of the most active First Ladies, traveling extensively and reporting back to her husband on the state of the country. Roosevelt was happy to spend much of his life serving his country. Like George Washington and Abraham Lincoln, Roosevelt's presidency took place during tough times when the survival of the United States was at stake.

President George H. W. Bush

The 41st president of the United States, George H. W. Bush was a veteran of World War II who served as a naval aviator and flew 58 combat missions. Bush was shot down by the Japanese in 1944 and he received the Distinguished Flying Cross. He graduated from Yale, created a successful oil company, and served in various government roles such as Ambassador to the United Nations and Director of the Central Intelligence

Agency. After serving as Vice president to Ronald Reagan, Bush was elected president of the United States. He served from 1989 through 1993.

President George W. Bush

The eldest son of George H. W. Bush, George W. Bush, was elected the 43rd President of the United States serving two terms from 2001–2009. After graduating from Yale and Harvard Business School, Bush went into the oil business and became co-owner of the Texas Rangers baseball team. Elected as Governor of Texas, Bush won the election to the presidency twice.

President Harry Truman

The 33rd President of the United States, Harry Truman, followed Franklin Delano Roosevelt. Truman fought in World War I and he learned a great deal about leadership in the service. He faced many challenges: Ending the War with Japan; helping to rebuild Europe; responding to communist threats; and facing a new war in Korea. Truman had witnessed discrimination against black soldiers returning from the war and he introduced measures that produced substantial change in the military and in civil service. Truman also recognized the State of Israel. Truman's presidential style was said to be unpolished, but honest. He had a sign on his desk that stated: "The buck stops here." It was his way of saying, he will make the decisions and you can blame him if you don't like them.

President John F. Kennedy

John F. Kennedy was the 35th President of the United States. Kennedy joined the Navy after graduating from Harvard. In World War II, he skippered the PT-109 (torpedo patrol boat) a small heavily armed vessel used for troop landings, destroying mines, and other work requiring speed and maneuverability. With Kennedy and his crew onboard, the PT-109 was sunk by a Japanese destroyer. Kennedy led his crewmembers to safety. In 1955, he wrote a book on bravery called *Profiles in Courage*, which won the Pulitzer Prize in history. Elected in 1960, Kennedy was an optimistic president who wanted all Americans to help society improve. In his inaugural address, he exclaimed: "Ask not what your country can do for you–ask what you can do for your country." Kennedy had many expansive ideas and an impressive group of advisers to help him get things done. However, he often found himself responding to problems of the Cold War. On November 22, 1963, Kennedy was killed by an assassin's bullets in Dallas, Texas.

President Theodore "Teddy" Roosevelt

President Theodore Roosevelt was the 26th President of the United States. Roosevelt was one of our most energetic Presidents. He was an author, a naturalist, soldier, explorer, and a historian. He was also a distant cousin of President Franklin Roosevelt and an uncle to Eleanor Roosevelt. Roosevelt won the Nobel Peace Prize and the Medal of Honor. His image is depicted on Mount Rushmore along with our first president George Washington, our third president Thomas Jefferson, and Abraham Lincoln. As a young boy he was sickly, but he took on strenuous exercise to become fit.

President William Howard Taft

William Howard Taft was elected 27th president of the United States. Taft served on the Superior Court of

Cincinnati and was appointed Solicitor General of the United States in 1891. He also served as a judge on the United States Court of Appeals for the Sixth Circuit. In 1900, he was appointed Governor-General of the Philippines and in 1904, President Theodore Roosevelt appointed Taft Secretary of War. After his term as president from 1909–1913, Taft became the tenth Chief Justice of the United States from 1921–1930.

Principles

Principles are the basic values or truths that we usually learn when we are young. Baseball principles are the basic fundamentals that coaches teach young players to help them play well and fairly.

Puerto Rico

Puerto Rico is a territory of the United States. It is an island group 1000 miles from southeast of Florida; east of Cuba, Haiti, and the Dominican Republic.

Roaring 20s

The Roaring Twenties was the optimistic decade of the 1920s in Western society and culture that featured economic prosperity with the development of automobiles, telephones, movies, radio, and electrical appliances. It would end with the Stock Market crash and the start of the Great Depression.

Rice, Grantland

Grantland Rice was one of America's greatest sportswriters in the first half of the 20th century. He wrote over 20,000 syndicated columns on sports. He was an elegant writer and sometimes wrote poems to go along with his stories. His most recognizable: "For when the One Great Scorer comes to mark against your name, he writes not that you won or lost, but how you played the game." Rice's autobiography is *The Tumult and the Shouting*.

"Round-tripper"

A round-tripper is slang for a home run. When you hit a round-tripper, you run completely around the entire base path touching every base!

Saint Mary's Industrial School for Boys

Saint Mary's Industrial School for Boys was the school and orphanage where Babe Ruth spent 13 years of his life. Students lived under strict discipline. Programs were established to teach working skills. Boys were encouraged to play sports and baseball was by far the most popular and important program.

Science of Hitting (The)

Babe Ruth once described his approach to hitting: "All I can tell you is I pick a good one and just sock it." That was not Ted Williams' approach. Ted Williams was a student of baseball and he argued that hitting a baseball was one of the most difficult things to do in sports. Williams sought advice from every great hitter and pitcher he knew. From that advice and his own experience, Williams wrote *The Science of Hitting* in 1970. The book has been updated since and it continues to sell to hitters today at all levels.

Scully, Vin

Vin Scully was the voice of the Dodgers from 1950–2016. Scully began with the Dodgers in Brooklyn, New

York, and when the team headed west to Los Angeles, so did he. While much has been written about the length of Scully's career, it would have never lasted so long, had his work been anything but decent, honest, and most interesting to baseball fans. No one has called the play-by-play for one team longer.

Self-control

Self-control is controlling your own feelings or actions—resisting any desire to act badly or thoughtlessly regardless of the circumstances.

Shrinking violet

A "shrinking violet" is an idiom that refers to someone who when faced with criticism or aggression is likely to cower or shy away.

Small ball

Small ball refers to a baseball philosophy for winning that focuses on small but important things like base hits, stealing bases, excellent base running, and moving players on the base path into scoring position.

Sphinx

The Egyptian Sphinx is a limestone statue of a mythical creature with the body of a lion and the head of a male human. Believed to be built about 2500 BC, it is one of the largest sculptures in the world. It is the oldest monumental sculpture in Egypt. We understand little about the builders and purpose of the Egyptian Sphinx. We know more about the Sphinx in Greek mythology who has the head of a woman, the haunches of a lion, and the wings of a bird. According to Greek legend, the gods sent the troublesome Sphinx to the earth. The

Sphinx tears apart and devours those who can't answer her riddle correctly. In the Sophocles play, "Oedipus Rex," Oedipus is said to have answered the riddle correctly thereby ridding the city of Thebes of the Sphinx.

Several sources reference the Sphinx riddle:

"What creature walks on four legs, then two, then three?" The correct answer: man, who crawls, then walks, then uses a cane (as he ages).

The Sphinx remains the treacherous quiz-giver in literature. And reference continues to be made of her.

Spitball Pitcher

To throw a spitball the pitcher applies saliva to the baseball to change how the ball flows through the air or to reduce resistance between the pitcher's fingers and the ball. Pitchers have also been known at times to use other substances to doctor the baseball. In the modern game, spitballs are illegal. This kind of approach is less likely to work with frequent ball changes and the umpire constantly checking the ball. Still, a few pitchers have been known to use the pitch in the last half of the 20th century.

The spitball was banned before the 1920 season, though some pitchers were allowed to continue throwing the pitch for the remainder of their careers.

Stepped Up to the Plate

"Stepped up to the plate" is what you hear a baseball announcer say as the next batter gets in position in the batters' box to face the pitcher. Stepped up to the plate is also an "idiom," an expression that means more than the dictionary definition of its words. Many idioms come from baseball. Someone who steps up to the plate is someone who is about to take action—perhaps to attempt to do something difficult or noble. Example: "No one at the parent teachers' meeting wanted to take charge of the cleanup crew, but Mrs. Stickler stepped up to the plate."

Stickball

Stickball is an informal baseball game played out on the street. Normally, it is a city game. The bat might be something like an old broom handle (or at least looks like an old broom handle as opposed to a baseball bat) and the ball is usually a small rubber ball. Each at-bat gets one pitch. The origins of stickball go back to when playing equipment was hard to get. There are stickball tournaments in various cities today and teams travel long distances to play in them.

Strike-out

Strike-out is an informal baseball game that requires as few as two contestants. Usually, strike-out is played against a diamond backstop or against a wall. Normally, a rubber ball is used. One player pitches while the other hits. The pitching "rubber" is often just a chalk mark on the ground. Home plate is often drawn on the ground as well unless play is at a baseball diamond. The pitcher throws attempting to strike the batter out. Three strikes to an out, three outs to an at-bat. Players devise their own system for establishing hits, fouls, and balls caught for outs.

Subjective

Subjective statements are those that are affected by our experience, feelings, points of reference, and backgrounds. Objective statements are those that are rendered by fact without any preconceived notions, feelings, or experiences.

"The shot heard round the world"

"The shot heard round the world" was a line from the poem "A Concord Hymn" by Ralph Waldo Emerson that was written to memorialize the Battle of Concord, the first battle in the Revolutionary War.

"By the rude bridge that arched the flood,
Their flag to April's breeze unfurled,
Here once the embattled farmers stood,
And fired the shot heard round the world."

The line has become an idiom meaning some extraordinary event. In a sense it is also used many times as a means of hyperbole to exaggerate the importance of an action or event as in Bobby Thomson's home run.

Tooth and Nail

The expression "to fight tooth and nail" means to give every effort to win, defend, or battle—the way an animal would fight for survival—using every means possible. Today it is used as an idiom to suggest extra effort given to obtain a result.

Town Ball

Town Ball is one of several bat and ball games that existed before baseball. Town Ball was played in some areas in the United States. Rules were changed and it developed into baseball.

Tradesmen

A tradesmen is a craftsman or someone who practices a skilled trade such as a carpenter or a plumber. A tradesman is also someone who manages a retail store.

Triple Crown

Triple Crown is a recognition that a player earns when he leads a league in batting average, home runs, and runs batted in (RBIs) over a full regular season. There is also a Triple Crown for pitchers. The Triple Crown Pitcher leads the league in wins, strikeouts and earned run average (ERA).

Unparalleled

Unparalleled is something that is unequal, distinctive, peerless—it is something that is not comparable with anything else.

Vaudeville

Vaudeville shows of live performances were often made up of different acts grouped together as variety shows. Acts included comedy routines, singing, juggling, ventriloquists, sports stars, dancers, impersonators, magicians, and more. Vaudeville was for the most part replaced with movies.

Vintage base ball

Vintage base ball is a bat and ball game played using early rules. Old-styled uniforms, and equipment are used today to demonstrate the history of baseball. The term for the game of baseball was often listed as "base ball" and hyphenated as "base-ball" before it became common practice to use "baseball."

Virtues

Virtues are those qualities that require us to act with excellence in conduct—the moral standard of integrity of character for the highest good.

"What's My Line"

"What's My Line" was a sophisticated game show that originally aired on the CBS Network from 1950–1967. Celebrity panelists questioned contestants to determine their occupation or line of work. For the last segment of each show, the panelists were blindfolded and questioned a mystery guest who was a celebrity. The show was hosted by news journalist John Charles Daly with panelists Dorothy Kilgallen (entertainment journalist), Arlene Francis (actress and radio personality), and Bennett Cerf (publisher). Many of America's cultural icons appeared as mystery guests.

Wilson Defensive Player of the Year Award

Wilson Defensive Player of the Year Award is a more recent award than the Rawlings Gold Glove Award. The Wilson Player of the Year is awarded annually to the best player at each fielding position in Major League Baseball. An overall Defensive Player of the Year and a Defensive Team of the Year are also selected annually. The Wilson Defensive Player of the Year Award winners are determined solely by baseball statistics or sabermetrics.

Wrigley Field

Wrigley Field was opened in 1914 as Weeghman Park for the Chicago Whales Federal League baseball team and later became the home of the Chicago Nationals owned by William Wrigley Jr. The Nationals would eventually take on the name Cubs. Wrigley Field is the second oldest National League Park and is known for its ivy-covered brick outfield wall and its hand-turned scoreboard. It is also the last Major League park to have lights installed.

Quiz

Here's a quiz on *Baseball's Winning Ways.*

1. Which president of the United States was responsible for the seventh inning stretch in Major League Baseball games?
a) Barack Obama
b) William Howard Taft
c) George W. Bush
d) William McKinley

2. Which president of the United States served once as president of the Texas Rangers?
a) Barack Obama
b) William Howard Taft
c) George W. Bush
d) George H. W. Bush

3. What famous book did Ben Franklin write?
a) *The Kite Runner*
b) *Autobiography of Ben Franklin*
c) *Common Sense*
d) *The Franklin Stove League*

4. World War I occurred in what century?
a) Nineteenth
b) Eighteenth
c) Twentieth
d) Seventeenth

5. What was Matthias Boutlier's occupation?
a) A catcher for the Yankees
b) A manager for the Cubs
c) An Egyptian paleontologist
d) A disciplinarian at St. Mary's Industrial School

6. Who wrote *The Science of Hitting*?
a) Babe Ruth
b) Honus Wagner
c) Ted Williams
d) Willie Mays

7. Who was president at the time of the Cuban Missile Crisis?
a) Harry Truman
b) Dwight Eisenhower
c) John F. Kennedy
d) Barack Obama

8. Which of these players did <u>not</u> play the outfield?
a) Joe DiMaggio
b) Mike Trout
c) Ty Cobb
d) Rogers Hornsby

9. In 1948, the Soviet forces blockaded rail, road, and water access to Allied-controlled areas of Berlin. How did the United States and Britain get food and supplies to the people?
a) They used tunnels.
b) They used tanks.
c) They gave up.
d) They flew them in.

10. What professional baseball player mentioned in the book is also a professional bowler?
a) Mookie Betts
b) Mike Trout
c) Nolan Arenado
d) Max Scherzer

11. What award is given to the player that "best exemplifies the game of baseball, sportsmanship, community involvement and the individual's contribution to his team?"
a) Brooks Robinson Trophy
b) Sandy Koufax Silver Cup
c) Roberto Clemente Award
d) Randy Johnson Gold Cup

12. The Flying Dutchman is <u>not</u>?
a) A nickname of Honus Wagner
b) An opera by Richard Wagner
c) A mythological phantom ship
d) A superhero of the Netherlands

13. What did <u>not</u> make Wrigley Field famous?
a) Hand operated scoreboard
b) Free gum to all in attendance
c) Ivy covered walls
d) One of the last stadiums to have lights

14. Stickball is usually <u>not</u> played with what?
a) A stick like a broom handle for a bat
b) A small rubber ball
c) A field that is out on the street
d) 11 players on a side

15. The Roaring 20s era was <u>not</u>?
a) A period of optimism
b) A time when automobiles, telephones, movies, radio, and electrical appliances were developed
c) A period of economic prosperity
d) A period known for conservative clothing.

16. Mike Trout is the centerfielder for which team?
a) New York Yankees
b) San Francisco Giants
c) Los Angeles Angels
d) Los Angeles Dodgers

17. Who is the all-time leader in no-hitters with seven?
a) Sandy Koufax
b) Clayton Kershaw
c) Randy Johnson
d) Nolan Ryan

18. Who managed the Philadelphia Athletics for 50 years?
a) Honus Wagner
b) John McGraw.
c) Connie Mack
d) Ernie Banks

19. Vin Scully was the "voice of the Dodgers" starting in 1950 when they were in what city?
a) Los Angeles
b) Brooklyn
c) Detroit
d) San Francisco

20. What was the U-2?
a) Wilson's best fielder's mitt
b) Poison gas
c) A Scottish Island
d) A spy plane

Exercise on Franklin's Virtues

Earlier in this book, we talked about Franklin's list of virtues and how he established habits using his charts. Like many of our founding fathers, Franklin was disciplined and self-reliant. For Franklin, his list of important virtues included temperance, silence, order, resolution, frugality, industry, sincerity, justice, moderation, cleanliness, tranquility, chastity, and humility. Some of Franklin's language may not be clear to you. Here is a brief explanation of his virtues taken from his autobiography and edited:

1. Temperance: Eat and drink sensibly.
2. Silence: Speak when speech is helpful.
3. Order: Have a proper place and time for everything.
4. Resolution: Perform what you ought.
5. Frugality. Spend only to do good to others or yourself.
6. Industry: Be employed in something useful.
7. Sincerity: Think and speak kindly/innocently.
8. Justice: Wrong no one and do your duty.
9. Moderation: Avoid extremes.
10. Cleanliness: Keep your body, clothes, and home clean.
11. Tranquility: Don't let small things disturb you.
12. Chastity: Be pure of heart and respect others.
13. Humility: Imitate unpretentious people (Franklin's example was Jesus and Socrates).

Talk to your parents about virtues that they were brought up with in their lives. Show them Franklin's list and work with them to create a list that would be important for you. After your discussion with your parents, write down your thoughts on living a virtuous life.

Discussion Questions

Discussion questions help you process information that you are learning. Here are some questions that will help you do that. These might be used in class, you might want to think about them on your own, or you might want to talk to your parents or friends to get their ideas as well.

1. Joe DiMaggio was successful in getting a hit in 56 games in a row. At the time, his hitting streak was the biggest story in the news. When the Yankees played, fans were glued to the radio or looking for the latest story on the Yankees in the newspapers. What are the greatest sports stories that you can remember?
2. It has been said that people who pay no attention to history, repeat it. Are there current events that you study in class that remind you of events in history?
3. Barack Obama came from a modest background, but he served as a community organizer, taught at the University of Chicago Law School, served in the Illinois State and the U.S. Senate, and served two terms as president of the United States. You may not know presidents or war heroes, but are there people you know who have overcome adversity to help others?
4. In President John F. Kennedy's inaugural address he challenged Americans with these words: "Ask not what your country can do for you—ask what you can do for your country." What do you think he meant? Would politicians use this message today?

5. Young athletes spend much of their time becoming better. Some go on to a sports career that pays well. They sometimes decide to do something for others. Roberto Clemente was one of these. He died in a plane crash delivering aid to earthquake victims. You may not become a highly paid athlete, but what would you do if you became successful? How would you give back?
6. Honus Wagner was called "The Flying Dutchman." Chances are that Wagner didn't mind the nickname. But about the same time, Fred Merkle was nicknamed "Bonehead Merkle" in the newspapers when he was unjustly blamed for a big loss. How do you react to bad nicknames?
7. In baseball, players would sometimes hurl insults at each other from opposing dugouts. Sometimes they came from the stands. People who are cruel to others can sometimes be encouraged by the laughs they get. What do you think would happen if people stopped laughing when others are cruel?
8. In America, successful people are allowed to keep most of the money they make and spend it on things they want. Most companies are like sports teams, they are highly competitive. Many jobs require workers to compete with others. Being competitive can be helpful in many jobs, but it is not so important in others. Think about jobs that you'd like to get and talk to your friends and classmates about jobs they want to get. Are the jobs mentioned those that require a competitive person?

9. In baseball there are many things you learn that help you in life. How we entertain ourselves outside of sports—TV, movies, and the arts, can be beneficial as well. Early television sitcoms might have been unrealistic, but they often had lessons to be learned or a good message. Today, many families' habits have changed. Some might play games, others tune into social media, and others might watch something on TV or another device. What do you and your friends think of the media that you consume?
10. In songs and literature, we are told that making the world a better place begins by looking in the mirror—we need to start with ourselves. Anyone can point the finger at others. We hope you have gotten some good out of *Baseball's Winning Ways*. Ben Franklin's charts might help you "look in the mirror." Will you give them a try?

CURVEBALL QUIZ

Name the famous Cubs All-Star who said, "It's a great day, let's play two!"

ANSWER ON THE FOLLOWING PAGE

[Curveball Quiz Solution: Ernie Banks]

Photos and Illustrations Credits

All photographs are reproduced with permission (unless public domain).

Page	Description	Source
Cover	Baseball Slugger	Bill Potter
Page vi	Author, J. D. Thorne	David Bernacchi
Page 5	Babe Ruth, John McGraw, Nick Altrock and Al Schact, Bain News Service	Library of Congress
Page 19	Josh Gibson and Homestead Grays, Harrison Studios	Wikimedia Commons
Page 32	Curveball Quiz: Derek Jeter	Bill Potter
Page 37	Christie Mathewson, Cincinnati Red Sox, 1916, George Grantham Bain Collection	Library of Congress
Page 48	Babe Ruth, New York Yankee, 1921, George Grantham Bain Collection	Library of Congress
Page 56	Justin Verlander	D. Benjamin Miller, Wikimedia Commons
Page 62	Christian Yelich	David Bernacchi
Page 64	Cy Young, George Grantham Bain Collection	Library of Congress
Page 73	Curveball Quiz: Connie Mack	Bill Potter
Page 92	Curveball Quiz: Cal Ripken Jr.	Bill Potter

Page	Description	Source
Page 95	Curveball Quiz: Randy Johnson	Bill Potter
Page 99	Curveball Quiz: Mike Trout	Bill Potter
Page 114	Curveball Quiz: Joe Madden	Bill Potter
Page 119	Benjamin Franklin, Maurin Lithograph of painting by Joseph-Siffrède Duplessis	Library of Congress
Page 121	Curveball Quiz: Molina brothers: Yadier, Bengie and José	Bill Potter
Page 133	Curveball Quiz: Mookie Betts	Bill Potter
Page 135	Curveball Quiz: Christian Yelich	Bill Potter
Page 139	Curveball Quiz: Greg Luzinski	Bill Potter
Page 178	Curveball Quiz: Ernie Banks	Bill Potter

Index

J. D. Thorne's Winning Ways

J. D. Thorne is an attorney and teacher who has promoted the good in baseball throughout his life in his writing, speaking, and his personal involvement with the game at every level. His first baseball book, *The 10 Commandments of Baseball: An Affectionate Look at Joe McCarthy's Principles for Success in Baseball (and Life),* is widely known and appreciated. Baseball fans and sports journalists have this historic keepsake in their homes and offices. Public libraries have helped carry Thorne's work to the masses.

A third-generation amateur ball player brought up with the game, Thorne was smitten with an early appreciation of baseball and all that it offers. Thorne writes to all generations of readers with *Baseball's Winning Ways*. Baseball history and entertainment are combined with biographies of current and past players. Also featured is an interesting ration of self-help that has been popular for hundreds of years! All is woven together to serve American readers on America's game. Thorne goes the extra mile to provide learning aids that make the book useful for those who want to use it in the classroom. *Baseball's Winning Ways* is recommended for all readers from junior high to adult.

Thorne is a successful labor and employment law attorney who practices in Milwaukee, Wisconsin. He is the author of *A Concise Guide to Successful Employment Law*. Thorne is a popular speaker and educator on the law and his favorite sport. J. D. and his wife Cindy are parents to three children: Andrew, Erik, and Julia; and grandparents to Austin and Jackson Thorne.